MORNING'S
AT SEVEN

DISCARDED

MORNING'S
AT SEVEN

by Paul Osborn

NELSON DOUBLEDAY, INC.
Garden City, New York

For
MILLICENT
JUDITH and GABLIELLE

The first Broadway production of *Morning's At Seven* opened on November 30, 1939 at the Longacre Theatre. It was produced by Dwight Deere Wiman, and directed by Joshua Logan, with sets designed by Jo Mielziner. The cast was as follows:

Theodore Swanson	Thomas Chalmers
Cora Swanson	Jean Adair
Aaronetta Gibbs	Dorothy Gish
Ida Bolton	Kate McComb
Carl Bolton	Russell Collins
Homer Bolton	John Alexander
Myrtle Brown	Enid Markey
Esther Crampton	Effie Shannon
David Crampton	Herbert Yost

Morning's At Seven opened again on Broadway on April 10, 1980 at the Lyceum Theatre. This production was presented by Elizabeth I. McCann, Nelle Nugent, and Ray Larsen, and was directed by Vivian Matalon. Sets were by William Ritman, Costumes by Linda Fisher, and Lights by Richard Nelson. The cast was as follows:

Theodore Swanson	Maurice Copeland
Cora Swanson	Teresa Wright
Aaronetta Gibbs	Elizabeth Wilson
Ida Bolton	Nancy Marchand
Carl Bolton	Richard Hamilton
Homer Bolton	David Rounds
Myrtle Brown	Lois de Banzie
Esther Crampton	Maureen O'Sullivan
David Crampton	Gary Merrill

Characters

In the House at the Left:
Theodore Swanson
Cora Swanson
Aaronetta Gibbs

In the House at the Right:
Ida Bolton
Carl Bolton
Homer Bolton

Others:
Myrtle Brown
Esther Crampton
David Crampton

Cora, Aaronetta, Ida and Esther are sisters.

Scene: Two backyards in an American town.

Time: 1922

Act I   Late afternoon in early fall.
Act II   Early the next morning.
Act III A few minutes later.

ACT I

ACT I

SCENE: The back porches and backyards of two houses in a middle-western town.

On the Stage Right is a neatly kept lawn with a few trees and under them a wicker chair. At back is seen the rear of the house, with windows on two levels. There are steps leading up to the porch. The lawn is bordered at Extreme Right by a hedge. This house and lawn take up four-fifths of the stage on the Right.

Stage Center is a path which extends back, separating the two lawns and the two houses and leading to the street beyond.

On Stage Left is practically a duplication of Stage Right except that the house is not in as good repair, the grass is not as neatly clipped and there are more trees and bushes, giving it a somewhat wilder appearance. It is bordered at Extreme Left by a hedge.

Exits and entrances can be made from either house through the back doors, from the drive between the houses and through the hedges Extreme Right and Left.

TIME: Present.

Although it is not yet dusk, it is evidently toward the close of a summer's day. Before the act is over it is dark.

AT RISE: As the curtain rises, Thor, Cora, and Arry are discovered sitting in the backyard of the house at Stage Right. Thor *is sitting on the tree stump Center, smoking. Cora sits on the porch ledge by the steps. Apart from them on the porch near the drive Center sits Arry. She is looking down the drive between the houses toward the street beyond. She seldom takes her eyes from the street.*

THOR

Then he listened to my heart. With one of those ear things. Didn't say a word. Scared me to death. Then he began to thump me. Chest, sides, back—all over. Still didn't say a word. Took my blood pressure. Oh, he did everything you could think of! Examination lasted over an hour. Then you know what he said?

CORA

What?

THOR

He says, "Mr. Swanson, there's not a thing in the world the matter with you. You've got a good heart, sound lungs, fine stomach —I don't know when I've seen a man of your age as well off as you are." Now what do you know about that? He's just a lousy doctor, that's all.

CORA

Did you tell him about your neck?

THOR

Of course I did! Said it wasn't anything to worry about! By God, I don't know how a doctor like that gets the reputation he has! Didn't even say I had to give up smoking!

CORA

Well, that's silly. Everybody knows you ought to give up smoking.

THOR

(*Disgusted*)
Of course they do!
(*Refers to his cigarette*)
It stands to reason when a man gets along in his late sixties he's

got to cut down on things like that! Well, I'll see old Doc Brooks tomorrow. He may be old, but I bet he knows enough to tell me to quit smoking.

CORA

You didn't say anything to the doctor about my side, did you?

THOR

By God, Cora, I didn't! I forgot all about it. Does it hurt you?
(*He rises—crosses to Cora*)

CORA

Just when I lean over.

THOR

Want me to rub it for you?

CORA

It'll be all right.

THOR

Well, you want to watch those things. Can't be too careful.
(*He crosses to chair Down Right—sits*)

CORA

(*Whispering*)
Thanks for asking to rub it, though.

ARRY

(*From up on porch*)
What's that? What did you say?

THOR

Nothing!

ARRY

Cora did. I heard her. She was whispering.

THOR

Well, she told me she didn't want me to rub her back for her.

ARRY

I don't see what there is to whisper about. When your own sister talks behind your back—

THOR

(*After slight pause*)
See anything yet, Arry? Aaronetta?

ARRY

(*Still looking down the street*)
What?

THOR

See anything yet?

ARRY

The Davises just drove by.

THOR

Which way they going?

ARRY

Toward town.
(*Cora produces a banana and begins to strip it*)

THOR

No sign of Homer and Myrtle?

ARRY

Not yet.
(*Rises and comes to head of porch steps*)
Dear, I wonder why they don't come. Wouldn't it be awful if he
didn't bring her after all?

CORA

Maybe her train's late.

ARRY

My, I bet Ida's excited!
(*Crosses Down and takes a piece of banana just as Cora is
about to eat it*)
I wonder if I shouldn't go over there and see if there's anything I
can do.
(*Starts cross Center*)

CORA

No, you stay away from there. Ida's got that Allen girl in to help her. If she wants us for anything she'll call us.

ARRY

Do you think we'll meet her? Myrtle, I mean?
    (*Crosses to Thor*)

THOR

Meet her? I guess Homer won't be bringing any girl of his home without introducing her to his old aunts and uncle.

ARRY

Well, there's something awful funny about it, if you ask me. How long has Homer been engaged to Myrtle now, Cora?

CORA

It must be nearly seven years. Of course they were going together four or five years before that.

ARRY

Well, don't you think it's funny, Homer's going with a girl for twelve years and none of us has ever seen her? Not even his own mother?

THOR

Well, Homer's shy. He can't be rushed into anything. Anyway, he's bringing her home now.

ARRY

Well, that's just because of that movie Ida saw the other day about the old bachelor. She said she felt so sorry for that old bachelor she came right home and gave Homer a terrible talking to. Said if he didn't bring Myrtle home she'd make him eat his dinners down town for a whole month.

CORA

Oh, she didn't either, Arry!

ARRY

    (*To Thor*)
She said she wasn't going to have any son of hers end up the way that old bachelor in the movie did.

THOR

Why? How'd he end up?

ARRY

He shot himself.
> (*They all giggle. Arry crosses Center and takes last piece of banana as she goes*)

Anyway, Ida's right about that old bachelor business. Homer's forty years old his last birthday, remember. If he's going to marry Myrtle he'd better do it pretty soon.
> (*Sits on stump*)

THOR

Well, I don't think Ida ought to rush him.

ARRY

Well, I just wonder what Myrtle thinks. I see myself waiting twelve years for any man.

THOR

You been waiting sixty-five years for one!
> (*He laughs heartily*)

ARRY

> (*Flaring up—rises*)

Don't you worry, Theodore Swanson! I could have had plenty of men if I'd wanted them!

THOR

> (*Suddenly placating*)

Sure you could, Arry.

ARRY

And they're plenty I could have right now too! Don't fool yourself about that!

THOR

Sure there are.

ARRY

I could have a home of my own in two minutes if I wanted one.
> (*Crosses to Thor*)

THOR

Don't doubt it for a second, Arry.

ARRY

I was the prettiest of all us four sisters, wasn't I, Cora?

CORA

No. You weren't as pretty as Esty.

ARRY

Well, I was prettier than you or Ida. And look at what Esty got.
Do you think I'd be married to a man like David?
    (*Crosses to porch steps*)
Trouble with me is I never saw a man who was worth the powder
to blow him up with. Pretty poor specimens on the whole.
        (*She is now half way up the steps. Puts her hand out for
        banana and finds it gone*)

CORA

You know what I hate most about this Myrtle-Homer situation?

THOR

What's that, Cora?

CORA

That nice house up there on Sycamore Drive that his father built
for them.

ARRY

That's five times you've mentioned that house in the last five
days. What's the idea?

CORA

I just think it's such a pity, that's all.

THOR

Yes, sir, by God, that's a fact. Five years that house's been standing there empty. All nicely furnished. I said to Carl just the other
day, "Why don't you rent that house until Homer's ready for it,
Carl?"

CORA

You did! What'd he say?

THOR

He says "No, Thor, no. That's Homer's house. I want it to be all new and ready for him any time he wants to move in."
> (*Pause. Arry rises and comes to top step. In a confidential tone*)

ARRY

Thor, you know what I've been wondering about Homer and Myrtle?

THOR

What?

ARRY

I wonder if there isn't something going on there.

CORA

> (*Sitting up*)

Oh, Arry!

ARRY

Oh, you can be as innocent as you like but I know what men are. Something could be going on there every night for all we know.

CORA

Well, I think that's a terrible thought to have about your own nephew!

ARRY

Well, it certainly could be true, couldn't it, Thor?

THOR

> (*Expanding*)

Well, it's hard to say. If it was anybody but Homer, I'd be inclined to say it could be. But Homer—I don't know.

CORA

Well, I know it isn't! Homer has never spent a night away from his home in his whole life as far as I know. He's always here in the mornings.

ARRY

Well, my goodness, he wouldn't have to spend the whole night, would he?

(*Suddenly the door of the house at Left is thrown open and Ida comes out hurriedly onto the porch and motions to Cora*)

IDA

Cora! Cora!

CORA

(*Rising and starting toward her on a run*)
What's the matter, Ida?

IDA

Come here a minute.

(*Cora hurries to her and the two step inside the screen door and stand there whispering excitedly. Ida's sudden burst out of the door has brought Thor and Arry out of their lethargy. Thor leans forward in his chair, and Arry crosses Center. They both watch with curiosity and excitement. Pause. The whispering goes on. Arry can stand it no longer*)

ARRY

(*Suddenly*)
Yap, yap, yap! When those two get together they're like a couple of old hens.

THOR

What's the matter with her?

ARRY

How do I know? Does anybody ever tell *me* anything?

THOR

(*Rising*)
Gee, Ida seems excited.

ARRY

It's "Cora, Cora, Cora" all the time! They just like to keep me out of things. She's probably burned her roast and I hope she has!

(*She crosses back to Thor and speaks in a low voice*)
And another thing, Theodore Swanson, the next time Cora starts
any more of this business about me getting a man and having a
home of my own like she did this morning—

THOR

(*Uncomfortable—sits*)
Oh, Arry, Cora didn't mean anything.

ARRY

Well, I don't know. Cora's made a couple of awful funny remarks
lately about me living by myself. She's got some bee in her bonnet. She's up to something.

THOR

Oh, she isn't either.

ARRY

Well, she hadn't better be, that's all I say.

THOR

Now your home's right here with us, Arry. Just as long as you
want it.

ARRY

Well, don't you forget it either.
(*Cora starts back*)

THOR

All right. All right. Now keep still. Here comes Cora.
(*Ida has gone back into house. Cora joins Arry and Thor*)

ARRY

Well, did you have your little conference?

CORA

Oh, my goodness, it's Carl! Ida says he's acting funny.

ARRY

(*Quickly*)
He's not going to have a spell, is he?

CORA

That's what she's afraid of. He's got his forehead leaned up against the kitchen wall and he won't move. Everybody's having to walk around him.

ARRY

(*Crossing Center*)
Oh, that's it, all right! No doubt about it!

CORA

Ida's nearly frantic. With Homer and Myrtle coming—

ARRY

(*Crossing back to Thor*)
And that's just what brought it on! Myrtle! Don't you see? He can't face her. That's the way it always used to be. Any new person he wanted to make an impression on—Oh, I bet he's going to have a terrible spell! I'd better go over and see what I can do.
(*She starts over*)

CORA

(*Grabbing her*)
You do no such thing!

ARRY

Oh, my goodness!

CORA

You stay right where you are!
(*At this point Arry is looking up the drive. She turns suddenly and calls in a hoarse voice*)

ARRY

Thor!

THOR

(*Jumping*)
Huh? What?

ARRY

(*Running up on the porch—Thor and Cora following*)
They're here! They're here!
(*Cora and Thor are back—Arry way out in view*)
Oh, my goodness, he really brought her! Look! Look!
(*She dances in excitement*)

CORA

(*Pulling her back out of view*)

Now be careful, Arry. Go up closer to the house.

(*They station themselves right in front of the door, and all huddle together, looking down the drive toward the front of the house opposite. Arry is nearest the corner, Thor behind her, Cora behind him*)

ARRY

Look! Look! That's her! That's Myrtle! Oh, Lord, he's helping her out of the car!

THOR

Yes sir, by God, he certainly is!

ARRY

Look! He's got hold of her arm!

THOR

By God, he has! Imagine that!

ARRY

You don't think she's a cripple or something?

CORA

Oh, Arry, he's just helping her.

ARRY

Well, he's certainly doing a good job of it—My goodness, look how he's got hold of her arm! You can't tell me there isn't something going on there!

CORA

We'd better go in. We can see better from the dining room anyway.

(*Carl enters from the other house. Thor sees him, but Arry and Cora don't. Thor tries to draw Arry's attention by nudging her*)

ARRY

Look! Look! Stop pushing, Thor. There they go—Stop it, Thor.

THOR

(Taking the bull by the horns)

Good afternoon, Carl.

(Arry and Cora look up guiltily and look over at Carl with a mixture of curiosity and embarrassment. They start moving away nonchalantly from their posts)

CARL

(Quietly)

Good afternoon, Thor.

CORA

(Crossing to head of porch steps and Down)

Oh, good afternoon, Carl.

CARL

(Crossing Center a bit)

Good afternoon, Cora.

ARRY

(At the head of steps. With an embarrassed laugh)

Well, I see you've got company.

CARL

Yes. Homer brought Myrtle for over Sunday.

ARRY

Oh, is that it? Isn't that nice.

(Pause. Carl stands there quietly. The others don't know what to do. Thor crosses Center—Arry comes down the steps)

THOR

(Heartily)

Well, begins to look as if you're going to have that house occupied pretty soon, Carl. Up there on Sycamore Drive.

CARL

(Trying to force a laugh)

Yes. Yes, it does, doesn't it?

THOR

(Encouraged)
Well, I'll be glad to see it happen. I always say all you have to
do is to leave young people alone and pretty soon things will take
care of themselves. Guess that's about the size of it.
*(Pause. Carl hasn't been listening. He has been staring past
them. Now he looks up quickly, noticing the silence)*

CARL

What's that?

THOR

(Lamely)
I say I guess that's about the size of it.

CARL

Oh!
*(He crosses to tree Down Left and puts his hand against
it and then leans his head on his hand. Pause. Cora, Arry
and Thor all stand watching him a minute)*

THOR

(In an awed whisper)
By God, he's having a spell all right!

CORA

Poor Ida! I'd better telephone her he's out of the kitchen.
(She goes in house Right)

ARRY

(Following up the steps)
I think we ought to phone Esty about it all, too. It's only fair.
Goodness knows she doesn't have much in her life anymore.
Come on, Thor.
*(She stands with screen door open. Phone rings. They exit
into house. Carl is still leaning against the tree. Ida enters
—doesn't see Carl)*

IDA

Carl!
(He makes no sign)

Carl!

> (*Still makes no sign. She sees him. Crosses to him*)

Carl! What *is* the matter? You're not really going to have a spell, are you? Answer me, Carl!

> (*She shakes his arm*)

Now you've got to stop this. Right away! Before it gets hold of you! You've got to shake it off and come right into the house with me and see Myrtle and Homer. They want you to come in.

CARL

They don't want to see me.

IDA

They do, Carl! They do! Myrtle asked for you especially. She wants to meet you.

CARL

Why should anybody want to meet a failure like me!

IDA

Now stop it, Carl! Myrtle is here. You've got to help entertain her. You know how hard it is for Homer to talk in front of strangers. You're the host, Carl. You just *can't* have a spell now!

CARL

> (*Straightens up—faces front*)

I never asked much out of life! Never made any demands! All I wanted to be was just a dentist!

IDA

Oh, my goodness!

CARL

I had a lofty ideal, but I never achieved it.

IDA

You're just as good as anybody else, Carl.

CARL

I failed.

> (*He leans on the tree again. Homer and Myrtle come out onto the porch at door Stage Left Center*)

IDA
(Pushing Carl Off Left—They both exit)
Oh, my goodness! They're coming out! Carl! Carl!

HOMER
This's the backyard.

MYRTLE
(Crosses to Center opening on porch)
The backyard! Oh, isn't it lovely!

HOMER
(At head of steps—points Stage Left)
That's the garage.

MYRTLE
Oh, yes! Isn't it nice!

HOMER
(Crosses Down—then Center)
That one's my father's and mine and that one's Uncle Thor's.
My father built them both.

MYRTLE
He must be terribly clever.

HOMER
He's a good builder.
(Pause—Homer points Right)
That's the hedge.

MYRTLE
(Following Down)
Oh, yes.

HOMER
That's where Aunt Cora thinks she heard a man hiding a couple
of times.

MYRTLE
Oh, that's right. I remember.

HOMER

Uncle Thor says it's probably just one of Aunt Arry's men hanging around to check up on her.

MYRTLE

Oh, maybe that's it.

HOMER

No, that's a joke.

MYRTLE

Oh, I see.
> (*She laughs at the joke, nervously. Sees Ida who is backing on Stage Left—looking Off after Carl. Myrtle steps toward her*)

Oh, there you are! Did you find Mr. Bolton?

IDA

> (*A bit flustered*)

I—I guess he must have gone for a little walk.

MYRTLE

> (*Looking Off Left*)

Oh, dear. I do so want to meet him.

IDA

> (*Blanking her view*)

Oh, he'll be back in time for supper. He often takes a little walk about this time.

MYRTLE

> (*In her best social manner*)

I love your backyard, Mrs. Bolton. It looks so cool. It's simply heavenly.

IDA

Yes, we like it very much.

MYRTLE

All the trees and everything. I bet you sit out here all the time.

IDA

We sit out here a good deal of the time.

MYRTLE

Well, I should think you would. It's simply heavenly. I don't know when I've seen a more attractive backyard.

IDA

Yes, we're very fond of it.

MYRTLE

Well, I should think so. It's so nice and wild, too. Like being in a forest.

IDA

I'm glad you like it.

MYRTLE

Well, I certainly do. It's simply—heavenly, that's all there is to it.

IDA

Well, it's nice of you to say so.

MYRTLE

Well, I mean it.
(*Pause. Conversation comes to an end abruptly—Homer steps forward*)

HOMER

(*Suddenly*)
Have mosquitoes sometimes.

IDA

Yes, there are mosquitoes sometimes.

MYRTLE

How dreadful!

IDA

But I don't think we've had quite so many this year as usual. Have you noticed that, Homer?

HOMER

(*In a loud voice*)
Not so many. That's right.

MYRTLE

Isn't it interesting the way those things go?

(*To Homer*)

One year you'll have a lot of mosquitoes and the next year not so many mosquitoes.

(*To Ida*)

Or a lot of caterpillars one year and the next year not so many caterpillars. I wonder why that is.

IDA

I don't know why that is. Do you, Homer?

HOMER

No. I don't know why it is.

MYRTLE

It's very interesting, isn't it?

IDA

Yes, that is interesting, isn't it, Homer?

HOMER

Sure is.

(*Pause. Conversation ends abruptly*)

(*Suddenly*)

Want to sit down?

MYRTLE

All right.

(*Crosses to stump*)

I'll take this cozy little place over here. Won't you sit down too, Mrs. Bolton?

IDA

(*Starting up steps*)

No, I really should be about supper.

MYRTLE

Oh, do sit down for just a minute.

IDA

(*Reluctantly sits in chair Left Center*)

Well, for just a minute then.

(*In silence they sit. Homer squats down and starts cut-
ting weeds with his pen knife. Myrtle and Ida smile at
each other. Ida on the edge of her chair. Short pause. Ida
rises*)

And now I really must go in.

(*Crosses to head of steps. Homer rises*)

I'll leave you two youngsters out here by yourselves. I guess you
can attend to yourselves all right. You probably have a lot to talk
over.

HOMER

We haven't got anything to talk over.

IDA

Of course you have! I know! I'll come out again as soon as I can
—If you should see your father tell him I want to see him,
Homer.

HOMER

All right, Mother.

(*She goes into house Left*)

MYRTLE

(*Sits on stump*)
Oh, I think your mother's too wonderful!

HOMER

She's pretty nice, all right.

MYRTLE

Oh, she's more than that. She's so—*human!*

(*Pause. Homer sits staring before him. Myrtle rises—
crosses Up of stump—looks at the house Right*)

And that's where your Uncle Thor and Aunt Cora live.

HOMER

And Aunt Arry.

MYRTLE

Oh, yes. She's the maiden aunt, isn't she?

HOMER

She's the old maid.
(*Myrtle gives a little nervous laugh*)

MYRTLE

How long has she been living with them?

HOMER

About forty-five to fifty years.

MYRTLE

My goodness, that must be pretty hard on your Aunt Cora.

HOMER

Why? They're sisters.

MYRTLE

Aunt Cora must be pretty nice, I think, to share her home like that.

HOMER

Aunt Cora's nice. Not as nice as Mother.

MYRTLE

Oh, of course not! Of course not. My goodness—Anyway it must be awfully pleasant for all of them to live so close together now that they're getting older. They must be a lot of company for each other.

HOMER

Then there's Aunt Esther, too.

MYRTLE

Oh, yes, Aunt Esther.

HOMER

(*Indicating with his finger*)
She lives up the street about a block and a half.

MYRTLE

And she's married to—?

HOMER

Uncle David.

MYRTLE

That's right. He's the one who studies all the time.

HOMER

He's a very highly educated man. He doesn't like us.

MYRTLE

Why not?

HOMER

He thinks we're morons.

MYRTLE

Morons? Why does he think that?

HOMER

I don't know. He says we don't think about important enough things.

MYRTLE

Does he think about important things?

HOMER

Practically all of the time.

MYRTLE

What does he do?

HOMER

Doesn't do anything now. He used to be a college professor. But he couldn't get along with the president.

MYRTLE

Oh.

HOMER

He said the president was a moron too!

MYRTLE

Well, he doesn't think *you're* a moron, Homer?

HOMER

He thinks we all are except my father. He says my father has

something more than the rest of us. Something that makes him
question life sometimes.

MYRTLE

Oh, I see.

HOMER

But the rest of us are all morons. That's why he never comes down
here and never lets any of us come up there.

MYRTLE

He sounds awfully odd to me.

HOMER

He doesn't let Aunt Esther come down either. He's afraid we'll
pull her down to our level.

MYRTLE

So she never comes down.

HOMER

Just when he doesn't know it.

MYRTLE

(Rises—crosses Left—takes off hat and leaves it on porch.
Pause. Myrtle turns to Homer)
Homer—do you think your mother liked me?

HOMER

She didn't say anything—I guess so though.

MYRTLE

It was terribly sweet of her to ask me to come.
(Pause. She takes a quick look at him. Steps toward him)
Of course I couldn't help but wonder why it just happened that
this time you decided to bring me. Because she has asked you to
before, hasn't she?

HOMER

(Uncomfortable)
Uh-huh.
(Pause)

MYRTLE

I mean I wondered if anything happened to change your mind.
    (*Slight pause*)

HOMER

    (*Suddenly*)
My mother saw a movie.

MYRTLE

A movie?

HOMER

Uh-huh.

MYRTLE

Oh!
    (*Pause*)
I guess she wouldn't think very much of me if she knew about us,
would she?

HOMER

Well, there's no reason for her to know.

MYRTLE

She'd think I wasn't very nice.

HOMER

Older people don't understand things like that very well, Myrtle.
Maybe we'd better not talk about it here.

MYRTLE

    (*Sits on ledge of porch steps*)
Oh, all right. Of course your mother must think it's rather funny
about you and me though. Being engaged so long.
    (*Pause*)
Hasn't she ever asked you anything about it? About when we're
going to get married, I mean?

HOMER

Uh-huh.

MYRTLE

What did you say to her?

HOMER

I told her you had a job.

MYRTLE

Oh!—Well, I was thinking about my job the other day. I was wondering whether I oughtn't to give it up.

HOMER

I thought you liked it.

MYRTLE

Oh, I do! It's a good job. But—well, I get awfully sick of it sometimes. And after all, I am thirty-nine years old, you know.
(*Pause. Myrtle stares at Homer. Nervously, he looks Off Left*)

HOMER

(*Pointing Off Left*)

My father set out most of these trees himself. Transplanted some of them. That one there I remember when it was just a twig he brought over from a house he was building on Maple Street. It must have been fifteen years ago.
(*Pause. Homer is staring before him. Myrtle looks at him, nervously*)

MYRTLE

There isn't anything the matter, is there, Homer?

HOMER

(*Shaking his head*)

Un-uh—

MYRTLE

You're not mad at me about anything, are you?

HOMER

No.

MYRTLE

You act so funny here. Are you sorry you brought me after all?

HOMER

No, I guess not.

(*Myrtle smiles at him and suddenly takes his arm and snuggles to him*)

MYRTLE

You silly!

HOMER

(*Pulling away*)

They'll see you from the other house, Myrtle.

MYRTLE

Oh!

(*She drops his arm. Pause. Then she rises and moves over by the trees Left—stands looking Off*)

I get awfully lonesome sometimes about this time of day. Or maybe a little later. I guess it's really not so bad at the office. I'm usually pretty busy. But when I get through and have to go to my room—And then when it starts getting dark—

(*Turns to Homer*)

Often when I know you're not going to be coming down I don't bother to get myself any supper. I just go right to bed.

(*They laugh—embarrassed. Pause*)

Sometimes I wonder how I ever happened to get stuck with that job. It doesn't seem natural. I guess when you come right down to it what a woman really wants is a home of her own.

(*Pause. Homer makes no answer. Arry wanders out from the porch at Right, casually, as though she were not aware of the others. They watch her for a time without speaking. She fans herself energetically*)

HOMER

That's Aunt Arry.

(*Pause as Arry looks Off Right*)

She knows we're here.

MYRTLE

Oh!

(*They watch her as she wanders Down Center pretending not to notice them. Sees a weed and makes a great fuss over picking it up. Then notices Homer and Myrtle, with much surprise)*

ARRY

Oh! Oh, hello, Homer.

HOMER

Hello, Aunt Arry.

ARRY

(Throwing the weed over the hedge)
When did you get home?

HOMER

Little while ago.

ARRY

Well!
   (Pause. Arry waits expectantly. As there is no move toward an introduction she bows politely to Myrtle)
How do you do?

MYRTLE

How do you do?

ARRY

It has been a pleasant day, hasn't it?

MYRTLE

Hasn't it?
   (Pause. Nothing more to say)

HOMER

(Suddenly—rising)
This's Myrtle Brown.

ARRY

Oh! Oh, how do you do, Myrtle?

MYRTLE

How do you do?

ARRY

I'm Homer's aunt.

MYRTLE

Well, I guess I know that. You're Aunt Arry. You're the one that sent me that handsome linen luncheon set for my hope chest.

ARRY

(*Confused*)

Oh, my goodness, that wasn't anything.

MYRTLE

(*Crossing Center*)

Well, I just guess it *was* something! That's about the most handsome linen luncheon set *I've* ever seen. Sometimes those flowers on the napkins seem to me to be absolutely real.

ARRY

(*Flattered—turns away a bit, laughs*)

They're appliqued, you know.

MYRTLE

I know they are.

HOMER

(*Suddenly*)

Myrtle knits.

(*Cora is seen passing the screen door, house Right*)

ARRY

(*Bowing pleasantly*)

Oh?—Haven't seen your father yet, have you, Homer?

(*Cora listens in door*)

HOMER

No.

ARRY

(*Crossing to steps*)

Dear, I hope he's going to be all right.

(*Homer looks up suddenly, startled. At the same moment Cora sticks her head out of the door*)

CORA

(*Hissing*)

Arry!

ARRY

(*Crossing to Cora*)

Oh, all right, Cora.

(*Sweetly to others as she starts in*)

I guess I have to help with supper. I just came out for a breath of
air.

HOMER

(*Rising abruptly*)

Where *is* Father?

ARRY

(*Crossing Down the steps again*)

I don't know, Homer. He and Ida were out there in the yard
when you came out. I just happened to notice them from the
house. He must have gone off through the hedge.

(*Homer turns suddenly and goes Off to the house. Myrtle
watches him, startled. She crosses after him a bit*)

HOMER

(*At the door*)

Mother!

(*Myrtle turns back to Arry who is nearly in the house
again*)

MYRTLE

Mr. Bolton isn't ill, is he?

ARRY

(*Crossing Center on porch. Confidentially*)

Well, no, he isn't ill exactly, but you see sometimes he has these
awful sp—

(*This time Cora comes right out onto the back porch*)

CORA

Arry!

ARRY

Oh, my goodness!

CORA

It's time to set table.

ARRY

(*Giving Cora a cross look—turns back to Myrtle sweetly*)
Well, I'm very glad to have met you, Myrtle. Perhaps we'll see
you after supper.

MYRTLE

I hope so.
(*Arry bows politely to Myrtle and starts in door*)

ARRY

(*In an undertone to Cora*)
I wasn't going to tell her a thing!
(*She exits—Cora has been staring curiously at Myrtle*)

CORA

(*Stepping forward—embarrassed*)
How do you do, Myrtle?

MYRTLE

How do you do?

CORA

I expect we'll meet each other after supper.

MYRTLE

I expect so.

CORA

Well, excuse me. I've got to go in now.
(*Starts in*)

MYRTLE

All right.
(*Cora turns back*)

CORA

I'm Aunt Cora.

MYRTLE

Yes, I know.
(*Cora bows politely and goes in quickly. Ida and Homer*

come out of house Left, and start down the steps. Homer
acts very moody)

Is there anything wrong with Mr. Bolton?

IDA
(Crossing Down to chair)

No, no, he just had a little headache is all. He'll walk it off and
be all right when he gets back.

MYRTLE
(Sits on stump)

Oh!

IDA

And I guess I can sit down for a little while now. Supper's nearly
ready.
(Sits on chair—Homer sits on porch step by Ida)

MYRTLE

It is? I had no idea it was so late.
(Rises—crosses to porch Left)
I think I'd better go in and wash up then.

IDA

Oh, all right. Just ask the Allen girl in there and she'll show you
where to go. The little towel with the escalloped border is for
you.

MYRTLE

Oh, all right, thank you. I won't be long.
(Myrtle exits. Homer rises—crosses Center)

IDA

Now, Homer!

HOMER
(Center)

I don't care, Mother! If he started talking about going back to
the fork again.

IDA

But I tell you he didn't. He didn't say anything about the fork at
all.

HOMER

Are you sure?

IDA

It hadn't got to that.

HOMER

Well, it hadn't better! If he starts talking about going back to the fork again—

IDA

Well, he didn't. I felt kind of sorry for him this time. It was one of those dentist spells. Now stop acting up and sit down. I want to tell you how much I like Myrtle. I think she's just as nice as she can be.

(*Homer sits on stump*)

HOMER

Well, I wish you wouldn't leave me alone with her all the time.

IDA

Now Homer—I

HOMER

I don't care, it's embarrassing. I don't know what to say to her.

IDA

Well, aren't you the limit. What do you say to her when you go down to visit her in North Lyons?

HOMER

That's different.

IDA

You are a goose, aren't you?

HOMER

Well, I just wish you wouldn't leave us alone. She keeps hinting things when you're not with us.

IDA

What things?

HOMER

Oh, she wants to know why I brought her home.

IDA

Well, I should think she'd know that. When a man brings a girl home to meet his mother—

HOMER

Now, Mother, you know I haven't made up my mind about anything yet!

IDA

Now Homer—!

HOMER
(*Shaking his head obstinately*)
Haven't made up my mind.

IDA

Well, when are you going to?

HOMER

Well, I like it living here at home.

IDA

But that's no excuse. And it isn't as though you'd be going way off somewhere. After all, Sycamore Drive is only half a mile away. You can come down here every night if you want to at first.

HOMER

It wouldn't be the same.

IDA

You'll be surprised how quickly you'll feel at home in that new house, Homer.

HOMER

But I've got all my things here and everything.

IDA

Well, I just wish you'd seen that movie I saw, Homer. That movie actor even looked a little like you.

HOMER

Who was it?

IDA

Oh, nobody important.

HOMER

Oh!

IDA

But he certainly gave you a very clear picture of just how lonely an old bachelor can be.
(*Pause*)

HOMER

(*Turns to Ida*)
You'd be awfully lonesome.

IDA

(*Turning away from him*)
Oh, I don't say it's going to be easy for me either.

HOMER

Of course it isn't.

IDA

It'll seem strange not to have you coming home after your day's work. But I've had you a long time. Longer than most mothers.

HOMER

I don't know what you'd do with my little room up there.

IDA

I think I'll keep it just as it is. Perhaps you'll want to spend a night down here once in a while—you and Myrtle.

HOMER

My room's too small for two people.

IDA

We might move in a double bed.
(*Pause. They are both rather embarrassed. Homer rises and crosses Left. It starts to grow dark. Homer turns back to face his mother*)

HOMER

Mother! Myrtle gets so personal sometimes.

IDA

What do you mean?

HOMER

Oh, she wants to know all sorts of things. The other day she asked me what size underwear I wore.

IDA

She did? What for?

HOMER

I guess she wanted to buy me some.

IDA

Well, that does seem odd.

HOMER

She wrote it down in a little book she's got.
(*Pause. They are both depressed*)

IDA

Do you love her, Homer?

HOMER

Well, I wouldn't want never to see her again.
(*Pause*)
Mother.

IDA

Yes, Homer?

HOMER

If I was to marry Myrtle do you think I'd—get used to it?

IDA

(*Faintly*)
I guess so—

HOMER

I don't know. Maybe I would. And you want me to do it so bad—
(*Ida is crying*)
Mother, what's the matter!
(*Homer crosses to Ida*)

IDA

Never mind me, Homer!

HOMER

Mother, you're crying!

IDA

I never thought of that! That she'd be buying your underwear!
(*She has a fresh burst of crying and gets up and starts toward the house. Homer pushes the chair back. Kicks the ground, disgusted with himself for upsetting his mother. He wanders Down to the tree Left and leans against it much as his father did. It has become quite dark. Thor comes out of the door at Right and stands on the porch. Suddenly he sees Homer and stares at him in amazement*)

THOR

(*Softly*)
By God!
(*He puts his head into the door*)
Arry! Cora! Come here!
(*Homer starts up guiltily, having heard Thor. Thor comes back out and looks over at Homer. He sees that Homer has heard him. Casually*)
Oh, that you, Homer?

HOMER

Yes.
(*Cora and Arry rush out of the house and stop abruptly at a signal from Thor. They stare at Homer*)

THOR

What you doing out there all by yourself?

HOMER

Nothing—I—I was just going in.
(*He starts up the steps Left*)

THOR

(*Crossing Center*)
Anything the matter with you?

HOMER

No—no—
> (*He goes into the house, hurriedly*)

ARRY
> (*Crossing Down with Cora*)

What is it? What's the matter?

THOR

Homer, by God! He was having a spell! I damn near thought it was Carl!

CORA
> (*Excited*)

What do you mean, Thor?

THOR

Had his head leaned up on that tree just like Carl does!

CORA

No!

THOR

Yes!

ARRY

Heredity!

THOR

By God, it is! It's heredity!
> (*Esther is seen hurrying Down between the houses*)

CORA

No, no, it can't be!

THOR

He was standing just like this!
> (*He turns suddenly and leans his forehead against the back of the house, his rear facing the audience*)

ARRY

That's it! That's it! Just the way Carl does!
> (*Esther appears*)

CORA

Here's Esty!

ESTHER

Good gracious! What's happened to Thor?

ARRY

Esty! Esty! Now Homer's got 'em!

ESTHER

Got what?

ARRY

Spells! Like Carl's!

ESTHER

(*Pointing to Thor*)
You mean Thor!

THOR

(*Disgusted*)
Naw, naw—Homer!

ARRY

Thor saw him standing right against that tree over there.
(*Esther laughs suddenly*)
Well, I don't see what there is to laugh at!

ESTHER

(*Sitting on the stump*)
Now, Arry, you don't really think Homer's going to have spells
too?

ARRY

I certainly do!

ESTHER

Well, I don't! I don't think Homer's got the gumption to have a
spell. He's too lazy.

CORA

(*Giggling*)

Of course he is.
> (*Esther laughs with her*)

ARRY

Of course you two smarties would know it all! And Thor saw him with his own eyes! Didn't you, Thor?

THOR

Well, you know it was kind of dark—maybe he was just kind of resting.

ARRY

Well, Theodore Swanson,
> (*Crossing up the stairs*)

if I couldn't live up to my convictions better than that—Men have no more courage than—
> (*Exits into house*)

THOR

Oh, Arry!
> (*He starts after her*)

I'll just go in and—I guess I shouldn't have said anything about it at all.

CORA

Oh, let her alone, Thor. Don't pamper her so!

THOR

No, I don't want her to be mad at me. Poor Arry! She's all alone in the world.
> (*He goes in. Esther rises and crosses to porch steps by Cora*)

CORA

> (*Disgusted*)

All alone in the world! The way Arry can always take Thor in—
> (*Turns to Esty—they smile at each other—both sit on porch steps*)

It's good to see you, Esty. You don't have to get right back, do you?

ESTHER

David'll be back from his walk in a little while. I want to be there
before he is. Carl hasn't come back yet, has he?

CORA

Not yet.

ESTHER

Ida phoned me. She wants me to talk to him.

CORA

Oh, I think he'll be all right. It's just one of those dentist spells.

ESTHER

Well, it's only one step from a dentist spell to a "Where am I"
spell, you know.

CORA

Why, Esty, he hasn't had a where-am-I spell in years and years.

ESTHER

Well, we can't do anything until he gets back. Now tell me. Have
you met Myrtle yet?

CORA

I haven't really met her. I just talked to her a second.

ESTHER

(Controlling a giggle)
What's she like?

CORA

(Giggling nervously)
Now, Esty! She's very nice! Not the way we imagined at all!

ESTHER

She has got teeth like this though, hasn't she?

CORA

Now, Esty, she has no such thing!

ESTHER

And she talks like this to Homer.
(They both giggle)

CORA

She doesn't either! She's perfectly all right. And we shouldn't sit here and giggle about it!

ESTHER

I can't help it! Somehow the idea of Homer's having a girl—

CORA

You know what Arry thinks? Well, Arry thinks that maybe everything isn't as straight there as it might be.

ESTHER

Well, maybe it isn't. Wonderful things can happen.

CORA

Esty!
          (*This sends them into a mild case of hysterics*)

ESTHER

          (*She wipes her eyes*)
My goodness, I haven't laughed so much for a long time.

CORA

That's right. How *is* David?

ESTHER

Oh, I don't know, Cora. He made me promise I'd never come down again without his permission.

CORA

You didn't promise him—?

ESTHER

Well—I—I really had to. He said—
          (*She gives a nervous giggle*)
He said if I ever came down again I'd—I'd have to live on the second floor the rest of my life.

CORA

Live on the second floor?

ESTHER

Upstairs. And he'd live downstairs.

CORA

If that isn't just like David! Why doesn't *he* live on the second floor?

ESTHER

He thought it would be easier for me on account of the bathroom.

CORA

Oh! Well, what would *he* do for a bathroom?

ESTHER

He'd have another put in. In that little closet off the kitchen.

CORA

(*Sharply*)
Well, *I* wouldn't pay any attention to him! David's just jealous!

ESTHER

I know it, Cora. He gets more so all the time. If he'd only stop talking about his Crystal Fortress.

CORA

You know, Esty, I always thought that Crystal Fortress was rather a lovely idea. Your friends or anybody can come up to the fortress and look in through the door—and you can see them and talk to them and everything—but no one can ever really come into it except just the two of you. Just you two all alone there by yourselves. It must be nice sometimes to be all alone with—the person you live with.
(*Pause. Esther sits watching Cora. Suddenly Cora turns on her and says with surprising viciousness*)
Esty! I hope Homer doesn't marry Myrtle!

ESTHER

What!

CORA

Oh, I know it's selfish of me! But I hope he doesn't!

ESTHER

But why, Cora?

CORA

Because if he doesn't, Carl has promised to let me have that house up on Sycamore Drive, to lease it to me for as long as I want.

ESTHER

But what would you want with that house?

CORA

I want to live in it! I want for Thor and me to live in it! All by ourselves.

ESTHER

And this house?

CORA

Arry can have it! She can have everything that's in it!

ESTHER

I see.
    (*Pause*)
What does Thor think?

CORA

Well, I—I don't know. I haven't asked him yet.

ESTHER

When is Carl going to let you know?

CORA

Well, Carl says that if Homer doesn't say definitely that he's going to get married while Myrtle's here—that is, set an actual date and all—well, Carl thinks Homer never will marry her and then I can have the house. I've got the lease all drawn up, right here. All he's got to do is sign it.
    (*She shows the lease in front of her waist. Esther looks at her sharply*)

ESTHER

    (*Rising*)
Well, I just hope it goes through without making any trouble for anyone.

CORA

(*Rising—suspicious*)
What do you mean? Who could it make any trouble for?

ESTHER

Oh, I didn't mean anybody in particular—I just meant—

CORA

I don't understand, Esty—

ESTHER

Shhh—!
(*Carl has entered from Stage Left. The lights have gone on in the house and he stops in the patch of light from the window. Puts foot on step, and then decides not to go in. Stands there*)

CORA

(*In a whisper*)
I'll be in the kitchen if you want me.

ESTHER

All right.
(*Cora exits into house Right. Esther starts across to Carl. He is so absorbed staring at the house he doesn't hear Esther until she is on him*)
Good evening, Carl.
(*Carl turns on her quickly and stands staring at her. Pause*)

CARL

Oh!

ESTHER

It's Esty.

CARL

Oh, yes—

ESTHER

I'm sorry I startled you.

CARL

(*Confused*)

Well, that's—that's all right, Esty—I was just—standing here—
        (*He becomes self-conscious and ashamed and to cover it
        becomes very jovial*)
Well, well, how are you, Esty? How are you?

ESTHER

I'm all right, Carl.

CARL

Well, it's nice to see you. Haven't seen you for several days.

ESTHER

No, I've been pretty busy with my garden.

CARL

(*Pulling chair up by porch steps*)
Well, come and sit down. How's David?

ESTHER

(*She sits—Carl sits by her on steps*)
David's fine.

CARL

Glad to hear it! Glad to hear it! Wonderful man, David. Wonderful man.

ESTHER

Yes, there're some fine things about David.

CARL

(*Carl suddenly realizes Esther has been staring at him.
Pause. He becomes self-conscious and embarrassed*)
Well—er—Myrtle's here.

ESTHER

Yes, I know.

CARL

Haven't met her yet. Guess I will at supper.

ESTHER

I want to meet her too.

CARL

(*Eagerly*)

You do? Well now, see here, Esty, you can go right in with me
and we'll meet her together.

(*He rubs his hands happily*)

Yes, sir, that's just what we'll do!

ESTHER

All right, Carl. Come on. Let's go in.

(*She starts to rise*)

CARL

(*Quickly stopping her*)

No, no. Not just yet. Let's wait a minute.

(*Pause. He is ashamed*)

Fact is, I sort of had one of my old—spells come on me, Esty.

ESTHER

Yes, Ida told me.

CARL

Guess I'm all right now.

ESTHER

Yes, you seem all right, Carl . . .

CARL

Yes. All right now.

(*Pause—suddenly drops his pose of joviality and turns on
Esther intensely*)

It's just that—just that—I'm not a stupid man, Esty!

ESTHER

I know you're not, Carl.

CARL

I'm not an educated man like David, but I'm not a stupid one!

ESTHER

Of course you're not.

CARL

(*Rising*)
Then WHERE AM I, Esty? WHERE AM I?

ESTHER

(*Rising—sharply*)
Now, Carl!

CARL

(*Excited*)
That's what I say, "Where am I in life." I'm caught, Esty!

ESTHER

Now listen to me, Carl—

CARL

I'm not where I should be at all! There's some other place in
life I should be! I'm *Carl Bolton*, Esty! The same Carl Bolton
I was when I was a boy! But now I'm sixty-eight years old and
WHERE AM I? Maybe I'm not Carl Bolton anymore at all!

ESTHER

Well, maybe you're not!
          (*Sudden pause. Carl stares at her slowly*)

CARL

What's that, Esty?

ESTHER

I say maybe you're not Carl Bolton anymore.

CARL

I don't understand. How could that be?
          (*Esty pats his arm reassuringly*)

ESTHER

Carl, you don't think you're the only one who feels this way
about things, do you?

CARL

Why—I don't know, Esty—

ESTHER

Well, I think lots of people feel exactly the same way as you do, only they don't go around having spells about it. You know, Carl, I don't think it's been any harder on you than on any of the others. Look at Thor—Arry having the whip hand over him all these years.

CARL

Yes, that's true, Esty.

ESTHER

I bet sometimes he wishes he were somewhere else in life too.

CARL

I guess he does, Esty.

ESTHER

And just think of all that Cora's been through. Never having a real home of her own.

CARL

Yes, that's true, Esty.

ESTHER

And Arry! Oh, well, I think Arry really loved Thor. I think she probably still does. Anyway, it's the closest thing to a husband she'll ever know. Come to think of it, Carl, I guess Arry doesn't quite know where she is either.
 (*Pause*)

CARL

Well, things get tangled up, don't they, Esty?

ESTHER

Don't they, though.

CARL

For everybody, I guess.
 (*Pause*)
I feel better. Lots better.

ESTHER

That's good. Shall we go in and see Myrtle then?

CARL

All right.
> (*They start toward the house*)

I always feel better talking to you, Esty.

ESTHER

Well, I'm the oldest.
> (*They exit into house Left. The Stage is empty for a minute. A man is seen to come from behind the hedge at Right and approach the house at Left, cautiously. He goes up to it and stands peering through the lighted window. Cora comes into dining room of house Right and starts to set table. Sees man and calls Thor and Arry*)

CORA

> (*In an excited whisper. All three come out on the porch*)

There he is! See! I knew it was someone!

THOR

> (*Calling*)

What do you want?
> (*He switches on the porch light. Then crosses Down. Man turns—there is a sudden shocked pause—then a frenzied fear seizes them all. They all speak at once*)

CORA

It's David! My goodness, it's David!
> (*She crosses Down*)

ARRY

> (*Yelling frantically*)

Esty! Esty!

THOR

> (*In a loud voice*)

Now look here, David! Esty's not here!

ARRY

> (*Yelling*)

Get out the front door, Esty!

CORA

Arry!

ARRY

(Coming to head of steps—crossing Down)
Well, he was looking in the window! He must have seen her.

THOR

I've been in the house, David. She might have slipped in when—

CORA

She was only going to stay a second, David. She was just going
home—
(Esther comes out of the house at Left, hurriedly. The
others freeze. David stands center, watching Esther. She
comes Down Left Center, followed by Ida and Carl.
Homer and Myrtle stay on the porch Left)

ESTHER

(Nervously)
Why, David, what are you doing here? I was just coming home. I
really was. Myrtle is here, you see, and I just ran down to—

IDA

She's only been here a minute—

ESTHER

You see, Ida phoned me Carl was having a spell—

CARL

That's right, David. I had a spell.

ESTHER

But I'm all ready to go now. Come on, let's—
(David has not moved. Esther stops suddenly and watches
him. He is looking at her. The others watch in silence.
Suddenly he looks at the group containing Thor, Cora and
Arry. They shrink back as he eyes them. He looks them
over slowly, from head to foot, giving each a thorough inspection. Then he looks at the other group. He gives them
the same individual, critical inspection. He stands a mo-

ment, throwing his head back in a puzzled way. He speaks
to himself as though he were trying to reason something
out)

DAVID

(Softly)
"And God created man in his own image; male and female
created he them."
(After a moment's thought, he gives a sudden shrug, as
though the entire problem were beyond him. He turns sud-
denly to Thor, as though seeing him for the first time)
Good evening, Theodore.

THOR

(Taken aback)
Good—evening, David—

DAVID

(Bowing pleasantly)
Cora—Aaronetta—

CORA

(As David turns to the others)
Good—evening, David—

DAVID

(More genuine)
Good evening, Carl.

CARL

(Eagerly)
Good evening, David.

DAVID

Ida—Homer—
(He hesitates before Myrtle)

HOMER

This's Myrtle Brown.

DAVID

Ah! This is Myrtle Brown. Good evening, Myrtle.

MYRTLE

Good evening. I'm very pleased to—
　　　(*He turns to Esther. Formally as to the others*)

DAVID

Good evening, Esther.

ESTHER

　　　(*Bewildered*)
Good evening, David—
　　　(*He bows to her formally and then surveys them all, smiling*)

DAVID

Well, well, here we all are together again. Our own little circle. I must say, you all seem to me very much the same as you always did.
　　　(*He beams on them. There is a rustling in the groups. They look at one another, bewildered*)

CORA

That's—very nice of you, David.

DAVID

Yes, just about the same. A little older, perhaps. Grayer. Pulses all a trifle slower, probably. But I can still see the same bright intelligent expressions on your faces that I remember so well.
　　　(*Slight pause as he beams on them*)
And now before I leave you there is just one thing more. You have all been in my home at one time or another. You all know how the entry hall leads into the living room and so is the entrance to the lower floor. And from the entry hall the staircase leads to the second floor. Well, now since Esther has decided it will be better for us to live apart from each other—

ESTHER

　　　(*Steps toward him*)
David—

DAVID

From now on, I will be living on the lower floor; Esther on the second.

ARRY

What's he mean, Esty?

ESTHER

(*Crossing to her*)
Why, you know David. He just talks that way!

IDA

(*Following Esty*)
What's he mean?

> Ad lib.

CORA

He told Esty if she came down here again
she'd have to live on the second floor.

ARRY

He what? He did not.

IDA

I don't believe it.

DAVID

(*Raising his hand for silence*)
Esther is a free agent now. She has a perfect right to come and go
as she pleases and to have anyone she wishes visit her. Doubtless
you will be there a great deal. Now none of you would come into
the lower floor, of course. But may I suggest that as you pass
through the entry hall and on up the stairs to be as—silent as possible?
(*Pause*)

ESTHER

But David, you don't really mean it?

DAVID

(*Surprised*)
That was our understanding, was it not, Esther? It seems to me it
was.

ESTHER

But, David, these are my *sisters!* They're all I have! I've got to
have something in my life!

DAVID

And now you have your sisters. Who am I to deprive you of that?

ARRY

That's what I say! Who are you to—

CORA

Arry!

ARRY

I don't care! He hasn't got any right to treat Esty like that!

IDA

I don't think he has either!

ARRY

Esty ought to be able to come down and see us any time she wants to.

CORA

After all, we are her sisters, David. It's only natural.

ESTHER

(Encouraged)

We don't do any harm, David. We just talk. I have a good time with my sisters. I don't care how ignorant they are!

ARRY

Of course she don't. Give it to him, Esty!

IDA

We're behind you, Esty.

ESTHER

I want to be able to come down here any
time I want to!   Ad lib.

ARRY

That's the ticket, Esty!

ESTHER

And I don't want to live on the second floor either!

IDA

Course she don't!

ARRY

Good for you, Esty!

CORA

She's got to have something in her life!   } Ad lib.

ARRY

Give it to him, Esty!
   (*They are all clustered around Esther, facing David, excited and angry. Sudden pause*)

DAVID

   (*Bowing courteously*)
Good night, Cora.

CORA

   (*Taken aback*)
Well—good night—David—

DAVID

   (*Bowing*)
Theodore—Ida—Aaronetta—

THOR

Good night, David—
   (*They all watch him, bewildered. He turns to Carl*)

DAVID

Good night, Carl—By the way, Carl, in the houses you have built you have also installed the plumbing, haven't you?

CARL

   (*Crossing to David*)
Why, yes, I have, David.

DAVID

I am turning the little closet near my kitchen into a bathroom. Do you suppose you could do it?

CARL

Why, I guess so—

DAVID

Would it be much of an undertaking?

CARL

That all depends on the bathroom upstairs. Is it right over the closet?

DAVID

Ah, that I'm afraid I wouldn't know.

CARL

If it is, it would be easy.

DAVID

Perhaps you would come up and look at it in the morning.

CARL

Well, I'd be glad to, David.

DAVID

Thank you, Carl. Good night, Carl—Homer—Myrtle—

MYRTLE

Good night. I'm delighted to have—
(*David has started out. He stops, turns*)

DAVID

(*Gently*)
You won't forget my little reminder, will you? About being quiet when you visit Esther? I say it out of the utmost kindness. You know, of course, without my telling you, how much you all depress me?
(*He looks from one to another, smiling*)
Yes—Well, good night, then. Good night.
(*He bows and exits between houses*)

THOR

By God! David can be awful nice when he wants to be.
(*Crosses to chair Right—sits*)

ESTHER

(*Crossing to the edge of porch—sitting*)
Oh, dear. I never should have come down here. It's all my fault.

ARRY

(*Crossing Up Center*)

It's not your fault at all! David's an old fool, if you want my opinion.

CARL

(Suddenly)
David's no fool!
(Quick silence. They all look at Carl, sharply)
David lives straight ahead the way he was meant to. He knows where he is. He didn't branch off.

IDA

(Crossing to him)
Oh, my goodness!

HOMER

(Pushing Myrtle in house)
Come in to supper, Myrtle.

IDA

It's time to come in to supper, Carl. Come along.

CORA

Go in to supper, Carl.

HOMER

Come in to supper, Father.

CARL

David thought it all out way back there at the crossroads. Then he went straight ahead.

IDA

Now stop it, Carl—Homer!

HOMER

(Joining them)
I'm coming, Mother.

CARL

He lived his life just the way he planned it. But I branched off.

IDA

(*Taking his arm*)
Come on now, Carl.

CARL

(*To Ida*)
Don't you see? I took the wrong turn. I got lost.

HOMER

Now get hold of yourself, Father.

CARL

(*Suddenly*)
I've got to go back to the fork!

IDA

(*Distressed*)
Oh, Carl, Carl! Don't say that!

CARL

I've got to take the other way.

HOMER

(*Trying to shake him*)
Father!

CARL

I've got to go back to the fork.

IDA

(*Her hands over her ears*)
Don't say that, Carl.

HOMER

Father, stop it! You're hurting my mother. You stop it now.
(*He shakes him. Carl stops suddenly. They have all been
watching, breathless. Suddenly Carl seems to come to himself. He sees Homer's attitude, sees all the others watching,
sees Ida crying, sees Myrtle staring in amazement*)

CARL

(*Trying to explain*)
I—I—I didn't mean—

(*Starts Left—speaks to Myrtle on porch steps*)
I didn't mean—
(*Turns to all of them*)
I just meant that I got to go back to the fork.
(*Exits through hedge Left*)
I've got to take the other way. I've got to—

IDA

(*Taking a step toward him*)
Carl.

HOMER

(*His arms around her*)
Never mind, Mother.

IDA

Carl!

HOMER

(*Comforting her*)
Come in the house, Mother.
(*Ida drops her head on Homer's shoulder*)

IDA

(*Sobbing*)
It came so quick—

HOMER

I knew it would. I knew he was working up to it.

IDA

And he's always going back to that fork—I never know what that
means.

HOMER

That's all right, Mother. I'll be here. I won't leave you, Mother.

IDA

Oh, Homer, Homer—

HOMER

Come in the house, Mother. Don't you worry. I'll take care of
you. There, there, Mother, there, there.

(*As he leads the sobbing Ida into the house Left, Myrtle crosses Down Left from the steps and watches them bewildered. The others have been watching and after Homer and Ida have gone in, all eyes center on Myrtle. Myrtle eyes them, helplessly. She gives a nervous laugh and falteringly walks up the steps. Again she gives a little laugh. Homer has switched porch light off*)

MYRTLE

I guess I better—

ARRY

(*Arry, deeply touched, takes a few steps toward her, wanting to do something but not knowing what*)
I—I—Myrtle?

MYRTLE

(*Stopping*)
Yes?

ARRY

I—I've just been thinking—I wondered—Well, if supper isn't quite ready I thought maybe—maybe you'd have time to see that quilt I'm making—

MYRTLE

(*Grateful, relieved—crosses Down to Arry*)
I'd *love* to see it.

ARRY

(*Taking her arm and leading her toward the house Right*)
It isn't finished, you know—There's more to be done on it—

MYRTLE

I'm sure it's beautiful—

ARRY

I hope you think so. You see—I didn't mean to tell you—But I'm making it for you—To go with the luncheon set—

MYRTLE

Oh, no!

ARRY

Yes, it's the same pattern.

MYRTLE

Oh, but I couldn't accept it—A *quilt!*

ARRY

(*They are going up the steps*)
You won't have to take it if you don't like it—

MYRTLE

I know I'll like it but—

ARRY

(*They are inside now*)
Well, it's yours then. My goodness, I certainly wouldn't have any
use for it—
(*They exit out of sight. Pause. Cora has been watching
where Homer and Ida left*)

CORA

Esty, Homer will never marry Myrtle now, will he?

ESTHER

Looks pretty bad.

THOR

Damn shame. Myrtle's a nice girl, too.

CORA

Well—
(*Light goes on in Arry's room*)
Esty, you just stay down here with us tonight and David'll come
to his senses by morning. You can have the bedroom downstairs.

ESTHER

(*Rising*)
I'm tired.

CORA

Of course you are.

ESTHER

It takes it out of you.
    (*They start up the porch steps and around Center*)

CORA

You're not as young as you were, Esty.

ESTHER

I guess that's it.

CORA

Besides, it's been a busy day.

ESTHER

Busy! It's been the busiest day I've had for a long time!
    (*They exit into side porch door. Pause. Arry comes out
    and looks around, suspicious*)

ARRY

    (*Crossing to porch edge, sitting*)
Myrtle's lying down in my room. I think she wanted to be alone.

THOR

Uh-huh.

ARRY

She's real nice, Myrtle.

THOR

Yup.

ARRY

Well, guess we better go in.
    (*Rises—switches porch light off*)

THOR

    (*Rising—crossing to porch step*)
Yup.

ARRY

    (*Moving back to front of porch. Stands looking at the sky
    a minute*)
'S going to be a nice night, Thor.

THOR

(*Turns and looks*)

Yup.

(*Pause*)

ARRY

(*Dreamily*)

Remember how bright it was that night we took the boat to—

THOR

(*Quickly*)

Shh! Arry!

(*He glances over shoulder toward the house*)

ARRY

(*Resigned*)

All right!

(*Suddenly bursting out*)

I get awful sick of having to keep still all the time! Sometimes I wish Cora would die!

(*Suddenly frightened*)

I didn't mean that, Thor! I didn't mean that!

THOR

I should hope not!

(*Crosses Up to porch*)

ARRY

I really didn't, Thor!

THOR

I don't like that, Arry.

(*Thor goes in abruptly. Arry stands a moment, alone, frightened. She looks up at the sky*)

ARRY

(*Frightened*)

I didn't mean that! Honest!

(*She hurries into the house*)

CURTAIN

ACT II

ACT II

SCENE: *The same. Seven-fifteen the next morning. Bright sun. Thor comes out of the house at Right. Is eating a banana, contentedly. Suddenly throws it from him.*

THOR

God, how I hate bananas!
      (*He moves Down to his chair and sits*)
Cora! I wonder where the hell she's got to? Arry!

ESTHER

      (*Enters from the Center porch door. Crosses down steps*)
Good morning, Thor.

THOR

Oh, morning, Esty.

ESTHER

What time is it?

THOR

About quarter past seven.

ESTHER

My goodness, isn't that awful. I never stay in bed that late. Is everybody else up?

THOR

(Sleepily—Esty sits on porch ledge)

Dunno, Esty. Haven't seen anybody. Just got up myself—Still, Cora must be up. She wasn't in bed—By God, the way she kicked around last night—you'd thought she had the measles or something.

ESTHER

Thor, what happened last night after I went to bed?

THOR

Well, seems Homer's broke off with Myrtle.

ESTHER

Oh, my goodness.

THOR

Yup. Told her it was all off. Couldn't leave his mother now that Carl was having spells again.

ESTHER

(Furious)

Oh, poor girl. Where is she?

THOR

Over at Ida's in bed, probably.

ESTHER

Poor thing. What an awful position for her to be in.

(Arry comes out of Ida's house—crosses Center)

Oh, there's Arry. Good morning, Arry.

ARRY

Good morning, Esty.

(To Thor)

Where's Cora?

THOR

I haven't seen her, Arry.

ARRY

Well, she isn't at Ida's and she isn't in bed.

THOR

Did you look on the roof?

ARRY

What would Cora be doing on the roof?

THOR

Dunno. She just might suddenly have gone crazy or something.
(*He chuckles*)

ARRY

(*Peeved*)
All right, you're so smart, listen to this. Carl didn't come home
last night.

ESTHER

What?

ARRY

He didn't come home last night, and he hasn't been home this
morning.

THOR

The hell you say!

ESTHER

How do you know?

ARRY

(*Impatiently*)
How do you think I know? Ida just told me. She's nearly frantic.
She wants to get out the Boy Scouts, but Homer won't let her.

ESTHER

Why won't he?

ARRY

Oh, you know how Homer is. He says it's embarrassing. It might
get around.

THOR

It's a hell of a time for Homer to get embarrassed.

ESTHER

Hasn't Ida any idea where he is?

ARRY

Of course she hasn't. He's probably wandering around the streets having a spell with everyone he meets.

THOR

(*Getting up*)
By God, we ought to do something.

ARRY

And another thing. Cora's gone, too.

THOR

What do you mean, "gone"?

ARRY

Well, where is she?

THOR

I don't know, but—
      (*Suddenly accusing—crosses to Arry*)
Now, look here, Arry, Cora hasn't got anything to do with Carl being gone. Cora was right in that bed with me all night—

ARRY

I didn't say anything about—

THOR

She kicked me every five minutes—

ARRY

(*Shouting*)
I didn't say Cora had gone with Carl—

THOR

Well, don't go making any cracks about Cora—
      (*Crosses Right—sits in chair*)

ARRY

I'm not making any cracks about her. But Cora went over to Ida's to talk to Carl. She was all excited about something. Said she had to see him right away. And when she found out Carl hadn't been home she ran out without saying a word. That was twenty minutes ago and she hasn't been seen or heard of since.

THOR

(*Uneasily*)

What did she want to talk to Carl about?

ARRY

That's what I'd like to know. Cora's up to something, you mark
my words. Last night when she found out Homer wasn't going to
marry Myrtle she got as nervous as a monkey. She's got some bee
in her bonnet, and if it's what I think it is—

(*Esther suddenly puts her hand up to her mouth. Arry
catches her and eyes her, sharply*)

What do *you* think she wants to see Carl about, Esty?

ESTHER

(*Innocently*)

Me?

ARRY

(*Imitating her*)

Yes, me!

ESTHER

How would I know, Arry?

ARRY

Oh, you make me sick. But I'll tell you one thing! If Cora is up
to something—and if it's what I think it is—well, some people
around here had just better watch out, that's all I say.

(*She looks significantly at Thor who squirms uneasily. Ida
comes out of house at Left*)

IDA

(*Mournfully crossing down steps—sits on ledge Left*)

Esty, Esty, have you heard—?

ESTHER

(*Crossing to her*)

Yes, Ida—

IDA

Poor Carl!

ESTHER

Now nothing's happened to him, Ida.

IDA

If we could only drag the river or something—
      (*Arry crosses Center*)

ESTHER

Now, Ida, there's no river anywhere around here.

IDA

He was always such a good husband to me. Never a cross word.
      (*Calling to Thor*)
Have you heard about Carl, Thor?

THOR

      (*Calling back*)
Yeah! Terrible thing, Ida.

IDA

He was such a good man.

THOR

By God, he was, Ida! That's a fact!

IDA

What do you think I ought to do?

THOR

Well, if it was me, I think I'd begin to look around a little—

IDA

That's what I think. But Homer says we don't want the whole
neighborhood to know.

THOR

      (*Rises—crosses Center*)
Tell you what I'll do. I know a fellow . . . Jim . . . down at the
police station—

IDA

      (*Horrified—rises and crosses Center—Esther follows*)
Police!

THOR

Sure. They're the ones to handle things like this. I could call Jim up sort of casually—not giving anything away—you know, and ask him what you're supposed to do in a case like this.

ESTHER

That's just the thing to do, Ida.

IDA

(*Hesitantly*)

But Homer says if anything had happened we'd have heard—

ARRY

Not necessarily.

(*Crosses to Ida*)

Just suppose Carl took it into his head last night to walk up on Randall's hill where he goes. And suppose he fell off that bad drop there. He was having a spell, remember. And suppose he knocked himself unconscious on one of those rocks—or even just broke a leg—why, he could lie there for weeks before—

ESTHER

Oh, Carl wouldn't fall off that drop!

ARRY

(*Crosses to her*)

In the dark he wouldn't?

ESTHER

No, he wouldn't. Carl's no fool.

(*Ida sits on stump*)

ARRY

Esty, sometimes you are the most exasperating woman I ever knew!

THOR

(*To Ida*)

What do you say, Ida? I won't give away a thing. I'll just say, "Hello, Jim. How are you? How're the kids?"

ESTHER

You might mention something about Carl.

THOR

Sure, I'll sneak Carl in.

IDA

Well, all right. But if it comes out all over the paper tomorrow—?

ARRY

(*Crosses Right—starts in*)
Come on, Ida. It's not going to get in the paper.

IDA

(*Rises—follows Thor up steps*)
Well, all right. But you be careful what you say, Thor.

THOR

By God, Ida, if Jim gets any idea of what I called him for I'll eat
my hat.
(*Thor and Ida go in house Right. Arry is still on the porch
—Esther sits on stump*)

ARRY

All over the paper! Anybody'd think Carl was running for Mayor
or something—
(*Notices that Esther has sat down*)
Aren't you coming in, Esty?

ESTHER

I don't think so. They don't need me.

ARRY

(*Hesitantly*)
I don't suppose they *need me* either but—
(*She takes one step down*)
You're not angry, are you?

ESTHER

(*Surprised*)
Why should I be angry?

ARRY

Well, I thought maybe I—spoke to you kind of sharp.
(*Crosses down stairs*)

ESTHER

(*Smiling*)
Oh! Oh, that's all right, Arry.

ARRY

I didn't mean to be—You know how I talk sometimes.

ESTHER

Yes, I know.

ARRY

I've just been all on edge the last few days.

ESTHER

Really? Why?

ARRY

Well, I don't know exactly. But there's something going on
around here I don't know about. And if there's one thing I hate
it's to have things going on behind my back.

ESTHER

Yes, you always hated that, Arry.

ARRY

For one thing it isn't polite. I like people to be open and above
board. When people start to sneak and—
        (*Cora enters hurriedly from between the houses. She is ex-
        cited. Arry turns on her sharply*)
Well, it's about time! Where have you been?

CORA

(*Anxiously*)
Has Carl come back?

ARRY

What do you want to know for?

ESTHER

No, he hasn't, Cora.

CORA

Nobody's heard anything?

ESTHER

Not a thing.

ARRY

(*Who has been eyeing her*)
What are you so excited about it for?

CORA

(*Flustered*)
Who wouldn't be excited about it?

ARRY

And where have you been?
(*Pause. Cora gets over being flustered. She becomes rather
superior, as though possessed of some secret knowledge*)

CORA

Well, I'll tell you, Arry. I've been for a little walk.

ARRY

You haven't either. You've been looking for Carl.

CORA

Well, my goodness, we've all got to do everything we can. I went
over to Ida's—

ARRY

That's right. To see Carl.

CORA

Yes. And when I found he wasn't there I thought he might have
gone up to Homer's house. But when I got up there, there wasn't
any sign of him.

ARRY

But what did you want to see him for?

CORA

(*Suddenly impatient*)
Oh, Arry, if I wanted to tell you that I would.

ARRY

(*Suddenly very dignified*)

Oh! Well, I certainly crave your pardon, Cora. I assure you I had no intentions of prying.

(*She starts toward the house*)

CORA

(*Sorry*)

Oh, it—it isn't anything, Arry—Don't get hurt.

ARRY

Please, Cora. I certainly wouldn't want you to tell me anything you didn't want to. I'll just go in and you can tell it to Esther.

(*Arry goes in*)

CORA

Oh, dear, now Arry's angry—Well, I can't help it!

(*She turns to Esther, excited*)

Oh, Esty, I'm so upset I don't know what to do! The first thing this morning I go over to see Carl—the lease all ready to sign—and he's gone.

(*She takes the lease from her blouse*)

I've put in here forty-five dollars a month. Twenty-year lease. I think he'll agree to that, don't you, Esty?

ESTHER

That seems fair enough.

CORA

Oh, Esty, isn't it wonderful?

ESTHER

It isn't wonderful yet. Thor hasn't agreed to it yet, you know.

CORA

(*Crossing to steps Right—sitting*)

Oh, he *will!* He's *got* to! He loves that house! Oh, Esty, I've never been so happy in my whole life as I am right this minute!

ESTHER

(*Rises—crosses to Cora—hesitantly*)

Thor may not take this just the way you think, you know.

(*Hurriedly*)

I mean—well, remember it isn't so easy to pick up and leave a house you've lived in so long—leave all the furniture and everything you're used to—so you know what I think?

CORA

What?

ESTHER

I think it might be a good idea to talk it over first with—Arry.
(*Quick pause. Cora draws back*)

CORA

Arry!
(*She looks suspiciously at Esty*)

ESTHER

Yes.

CORA

(*In a hard voice*)
Why? What business is it of hers?

ESTHER

It is her business in a way.

CORA

I don't see how.

ESTHER

Well, she's always lived with you. You're the only home she's ever known. You can't say she's not concerned.

CORA

I don't care if she is concerned. Thor is *my* husband, Esty.

ESTHER

Of course, Cora—I just thought—

CORA

(*With a slight sneer*)
You just thought nothing—
(*She crosses Center*)

ESTHER

But, Cora—

(*Thor comes out, followed by Ida and Arry. Cora hurriedly slips the lease into her waist although a small part of it shows*)

IDA

But what's the next step for us to take, Thor?

THOR

(*Coming down the steps, followed by Ida. Arry stays on the porch*)

By God, Ida, you got me. If you won't let me tell the police who Carl is—They can't very well start looking for somebody they don't know.

(*Esty sits on stump*)

ESTHER

What did they tell you, Thor?

THOR

They said to give a description of him.

ESTHER

I should think you could do that.

THOR

Ida says I can't.

IDA

(*Nervously—crosses to Esty*)

Well, Esty, Homer says—

CORA

(*Up Right Center—sweetly*)

Good morning, Thor.

THOR

What've you been up to this morning?

CORA

Me? Nothing at all.

IDA

Did you see anything of Carl?

CORA

Not a thing, Ida.

THOR

What'd you want to see Carl in such a hurry about?

CORA

I just wanted to find him for Ida.

ARRY

(*On porch just above Cora—laughing*)
That's very funny. Very funny.
(*She changes to a matter-of-fact voice*)
And what's this sticking out of your waist?
(*Pulls the lease*)

CORA

(*Slapping her hand*)
You keep your hands to yourself.

ARRY

Well, what is it?

CORA

None of your business.

ARRY

Hoity-toity!
(*Arry moves Up on the porch—but during the following scene eyes Cora intently*)

IDA

Maybe if we just gave a description without giving his name—

THOR

Sure! No use giving his name. Just his description. Sixty-six years old—

IDA

Sixty-eight, Thor.

THOR

Sixty-*eight*? Are you sure?

IDA

Well, I—I thought I was. Sixty-eight, isn't it, Esty?

ESTHER

Let's see. I'm seventy-two. And Cora's two years younger than I—

CORA

That's right. And Ida's four years younger than me.

IDA

Sixty-six, that's right. And Carl's two years older—

ESTHER

Sixty-eight.

THOR

Well, what the hell do you know about that! I wouldn't have said Carl was a day over sixty-six. By God, we're certainly getting along, this crowd.
      (*Hearty laugh*)

IDA
      (*Crossing porch ledge, Left—sits*)
Yes, sir, we certainly are.

THOR

We're certainly not getting any younger. And by God, I'm glad we're not. When I think how I used to go to that office every day at eight o'clock—

CORA

You never used to mind that so much, Thor.

THOR

Well, I'd mind it now.

ESTHER

Still, if you were getting younger you'd get back to the age where you wouldn't mind it.

THOR

What's that, Esty?

ESTHER

I say if you were forty again you wouldn't mind going to the office.

THOR

I'm not forty though.

ESTHER

But if you were getting younger you'd get back to forty.

THOR

(*Looking at her*)
What the hell are you talking about, Esty?

ESTHER

Never mind—anyway, blue eyes.
(*Arry gets down off the porch and starts slowly toward Cora*)

IDA

What's that, Esty?

ESTHER

Carl.

IDA

Oh, yes, Carl.

ESTHER

He's got blue eyes.

IDA

Oh!—Yes, that's right. Blue eyes.

THOR

(*Slight pause. He looks up at Ida, puzzled*)
Carl doesn't have blue eyes.

IDA

Yes, he does, Thor.

THOR

You sure? I thought Carl had brown eyes.

CORA

No, he doesn't either, Thor. Carl has blue eyes.

THOR

Really? Well, that just goes to show. You look at a thing and you
look at it and still you don't see it. I'm going to get a good square
look at Carl the next time I see him.

IDA

(*Tearfully*)
If you ever have a chance to see him.

THOR

Oh, by God, Ida, I'm sorry, I forgot.
> (*Arry has been circling closer and closer. At this point she
> is near enough to Cora to make a quick dive for the paper.
> She gets it and starts racing across the lawn as fast as she
> can go. Cora is on her feet in an instant and after her,
> shrieking. Thor sits up, startled*)

CORA

Arry! You give that back! You come back here with that paper.
Arry!
> (*A race ensues in which Arry, running as hard as she can,
> tries to get the paper out of the envelope and read it*)

Catch her! Head her off!
> (*Ida heads her off from going in the house*)

ESTHER

Give her back that paper, Arry!

THOR

What the hell's going on here?

CORA

You dare read that paper and I'll fix you, Aaronetta Gibbs!

ESTHER

You stop, Arry! Stop!

IDA

> (*Suddenly entering into the spirit of the thing*)

Look out, Arry, Cora's gaining on you.

THOR

What are they doing?

IDA

(*Laughing*)
I don't know. Arry's got something of Cora's.
(*Shouting*)
Look out, Arry.
(*They are all shrieking, ad lib. Arry races Right and gets
cornered by Ida Right—Esty Center—and Cora coming
after her from the Left—They are at the height of their
shrieking and pulling at each other as David enters Left.
The noise subsides. Even Arry quiets down and with a
final jerk, Cora gets the paper. Esther, in utter confusion,
faces David, weakly. David surveys them, smiling*)

DAVID

(*Pleasantly*)
Playing tag?

ESTHER

No, no—we were just—

DAVID

But don't apologize, Esther. You are a free agent now. You can
amuse yourself any way you wish.

ESTHER

But you don't understand, David—

DAVID

Please go on with the game. Don't let me interrupt you—

ESTHER

But we weren't playing a game. We were—

DAVID

(*Calling Off Left*)
I'll go in and wait for you in your room, Carl.
(*Starts up steps of house Left*)

CARL (Offstage)

All right, David.

EVERYBODY

Carl!

ESTHER

David!

(*She follows him into house. Carl, loaded down with tools, enters Left. Ida crosses to him*)

IDA

Carl!

CARL

(*Puts down bags*)
Oh, Ida—I hope you haven't been worried, Ida.

IDA

Worried! My goodness, Carl, I've been nearly frantic! Where have you been? What's the matter? Are you all right? Are you hurt?

CARL

(*Surprised*)
Hurt?

IDA

But where have you been, Carl? You stayed out all night. I've been nearly frantic. We even called the police.

CARL

Police?

IDA

We thought you might be dead!

CARL

Dead? No.

IDA

You didn't come home all night. I've been nearly frantic. Where have you been, Carl?

CARL

(*Surprised she doesn't know*)
Why, I've been up at David's.

IDA

But where did you sleep?

CARL

Well, we didn't sleep, Ida—we talked. David's going to help me find out where I am. We're right in the middle of it now. We just stopped long enough to come down and get my tools and pack my clothes—

IDA

Pack your clothes?

CARL

Yes, I—
   (*Realizes she doesn't understand*)
Oh! You see, I'm moving, Ida.

IDA

What do you mean?

CARL

Well, David has invited me to live with him. He wants me to.

IDA

Live with David?

CARL

   (*Crossing Left Center*)
Yes. You see, we're going to live on the lower floor. We're going to put in a real bath instead of just a seat and a basin and we're going to use the side entrance and—

IDA

What are you talking about, Carl?

CARL

   (*Turns to her—as to a child*)
I'm going to live with David for a while.

IDA

But what about *me*?

CARL

   (*Blankly*)
You?

IDA

Yes, *me*, Carl.

CARL

Oh, that's right. Well, you can live here just the way you do now.

IDA

You don't mean you're going to leave me, Carl?

CARL

But, I've lived here a long time, Ida. I want to live somewhere else for a while. You'll be all right. You've got Homer.

IDA

I just don't understand—

CARL

(*Crossing to pick up tools*)
I'll explain it to you sometime, Ida. I'll come down and see you—
(*David calls from inside house*)

DAVID

We're wasting valuable time, Carl.

CARL

(*Briskly—going in*)
Be right there, David. Be right there.

IDA

Carl! I've got to talk to you, Carl—
(*Follows him—Arry, Thor and Cora are watching*)

THOR

Well, what the hell do you know about that.

ARRY

I always knew that marriage wouldn't last—Anyway, Carl *has* got blue eyes.

THOR

There you are! Damn it all, I forgot to look again!
(*Crosses back to chair Right—sits*)

CORA

(*Starting Left*)
Well, I've got to run over and see him.

ARRY

(*Suddenly pulling Cora around*)
Oh, you do, eh! What for?
(*Sudden pause. They revert to their old tension*)

CORA

If you ask me that again, Arry, I'll—

THOR

That's right. What the hell's the matter with you two?

ARRY

What's in the paper, is what I want to know.

THOR

Whose paper is it?

ARRY

Cora's. She's been hiding it.

THOR

What business is it of yours then?

ARRY

Cora's up to something and I know it.

CORA

(*Hard*)
You want to know what's in this paper, Arry?

ARRY

Yes, I do!
(*Pause. Cora glares at Arry. She hands her the paper*)

CORA

(*In a hard voice*)
All right, look for yourself.
(*She gives Arry the paper. Arry reads it and looks up slowly. They eye each other in silence*)

THOR

(*Impatiently*)

Well, what is it?

(*Cora takes the paper and gives it to Thor. He reads it as Arry watches Cora, trying to figure out exactly what it means. Thor looks up, puzzled*)

This here's a twenty-year lease on Homer's house.

CORA

(*Steadily*)

Yes.

THOR

It's made out to you.

CORA

Yes.

THOR

What's it for?

ARRY

That's what I want to know.

THOR

Look here, Cora, what's the big idea?

CORA

(*After a moment*)

I'm going to rent it for us, Thor.

THOR

Us? What do we want with it?

CORA

You like that house, don't you, Thor?

THOR

Of course I like it but—

CORA

You like it better than this one, don't you?

THOR

What if I do? That's no reason to rent it.

CORA

Listen, Thor. We haven't got many years left ahead of us, have
we?

THOR

What's that got to do with it?

CORA

Everything. I want for the rest of the years we *have* got for you
and me to move up there and live together in that nice house.
Have a real home of our own.

THOR

(*Frightened*)
Now, look here, Cora, I don't know what you're getting at.

ARRY

I know what she's getting at.

CORA

There's no reason in the world that I can see why we can't do it.
Carl has promised to sign the lease. We can afford it. And we'd
love it. Just you and me—alone.

THOR

(*Rises*)
Good Lord, Cora, now look here—

CORA

(*Steadily*)
I've thought it all out, Thor. We can give this house to Arry. We
can make out some kind of transfer and she can own it in her
own name. She won't be lonesome with Ida and Esty here. And
we can have what's left of the years together—alone—as we
should always have had them in the past.

THOR

(*Horrified*)
Cora!

(Slight pause. Arry turns quickly and runs into the house)

Arry—

(He takes a step toward her and then turns back. Cora is watching him)

By God, Cora, how could you say a thing like that?

CORA

(Crosses Center a step—steadily)

It's the truth, isn't it?

THOR

But right in front of Arry.

CORA

She had it coming to her.

THOR

But think how she must feel.

CORA

I know how she feels—Well, what about it, Thor? Shall we do it?

THOR

(Uneasily)

But we can't do a thing like that—

CORA

Why not?

THOR

We just couldn't. It wouldn't be fair to Arry. Poor Arry, she's all alone in the world.

CORA

So am I. You can be alone a lot of different ways, Thor.

THOR

And Carl isn't going to rent that house—

CORA

If he doesn't, then we can't do it. But if he does, are you willing?

THOR

But Cora—

CORA

You're not afraid, are you, Thor?

THOR

Afraid? Afraid of what?

CORA

Of anything.

THOR

(*Uneasily*)
I don't know what you mean.

CORA

All right. Then you think it over, Thor, will you?

THOR

(*Same*)
I guess—I can think it over—

CORA

(*Crossing Left to Ida's house*)
Thank you—Now I'm going over to Ida's and talk to Carl. I
think we can get that house, Thor.

THOR

(*Crossing Center—afraid*)
Don't do it now, Cora. Wait till we talk it over.

CORA

(*On steps*)
No, Carl may get away again. We don't want to take any
chances.
(*She exits into house*)

THOR

(*Desperate*)
But—
(*Arry enters from house Right. Thor turns*)
Gee, Arry, I'm so sorry about that. Cora didn't mean anything—

ARRY

She meant it all right.

THOR

She was just mad. I'm sorry as I can be.

ARRY

No use being sorry. The point is what are you going to do about it? If Cora gets that house are you going to move up there?

THOR

(*At stump*)
Of course not, Arry—

ARRY

How will you get out of it?

THOR

I'll talk to Cora and—

ARRY

What will you tell her?

THOR

(*Sits on stump*)
I'll fix it up some way.

ARRY

She's over seeing Carl now. Why didn't you stop her?

THOR

I couldn't just then—

ARRY

You listened to Cora. Now you listen to me, Thor. Cora can talk about having what's left of her life alone with you. Well, what about me? How many years do you think I've got left?

THOR

I know, Arry, I know—

ARRY

And whose fault is it that *I* haven't got a home of my own?

THOR

All right, Arry. Now your home's right here with us—

ARRY

I've got just as much right here as Cora.

THOR

Now be quiet, Arry. I'll think of something.

ARRY

You'd better. Because I'm not going to spend the rest of my life alone. After all I've given up.

THOR

I don't think Carl'll give her the house anyway.

ARRY

Well, if he does, and you leave me now, Thor, don't think I won't tell what's happened. I'm not ashamed. I'd *like* to have Cora know.

THOR

(*Sharply*)
Now keep still, Arry.

ARRY

All right. But don't think Cora's going to make it easy for you. You'd better think up something pretty good, Thor.
(*She starts in—stops on top step*)
You didn't have much breakfast this morning, did you?

THOR

(*Abused*)
I had a banana.

ARRY

Well, come in. I'll fix you something.
(*She goes in. Thor starts in, gloomily*)

THOR

Doggone it all!
(*As he starts in, Homer comes out of house Left, furious—*

*he slams porch door—starts around Center on porch—
then sees Thor. Thor speaks gloomily)*
'Morning, Homer.

HOMER

(Stops pacing)
'Morning, Uncle Thor.
    (Continues pacing—suddenly stops and looks up, furious)
Aunt Cora got my house away from me!

THOR

(Quickly)
What's that?

HOMER

While I was shaving!

THOR

What do you mean, Homer?

HOMER

I was upstairs shaving and when I came down my father had
rented my house to Aunt Cora.

THOR

You mean he signed the lease?

HOMER

Just as I was coming downstairs.

THOR

Oh, my God!
    *(Thor exits into house Right—Ida comes out of house
Left—follows Homer Down Center)*

IDA

Homer—Oh, Homer, I'm so sorry about it!

HOMER

(Moving away)
I don't want to talk about it, Mother. I've got to think.

IDA

Do you feel awfully bad?

HOMER

How do you think I feel? How would you feel if you suddenly found out you didn't have a house anymore? That was *my* house. Myrtle's and mine.

(*Crosses to chair Left Center*)

IDA

Yes, it was, Homer, but—

HOMER

(*Sits*)

And now it's not my house anymore. Now Myrtle and I haven't got a house anymore.

IDA

I don't suppose Carl thought you'd care—You and Myrtle weren't going to use it—

HOMER

We go up and look at it, don't we? We talk to each other about it. Now what are we going to talk about?

IDA

But you said you weren't going to get married and—

HOMER

I didn't say we weren't engaged.

IDA

Oh, dear, I'd do anything to get it back for you. I've never seen Cora so stubborn about anything. She won't even talk about it. She's calling up the electric company right now to have the lights turned on.

HOMER

What I'm going to say to Myrtle when she gets up, I don't know. It'll just about break her heart. She makes plans about that house all the time. She's told all her friends down in North Lyons about her beautiful house. Well, now she hasn't got one anymore. We just took it away from her. Pretty small business, I must say! Invite a girl to stay over night and then take her house away from

her when she's asleep. Pretty small business! *I* don't know what
the world's coming to.

IDA

Well, I'll talk to Carl about it just as soon as I can. He and
David have locked themselves in the bedroom until they're
finished packing and won't talk to us, but as soon as they come
out I'll—

HOMER

That won't do any good. He can't do anything. No, my house is
gone, Mother. It's just gone.

IDA

(*Distressed—sits on stump*)
Oh, Homer, I'm so sorry—

HOMER

(*Suddenly—rising*)
What's it all about, that's what I ask myself!

IDA

What's what all about, Homer?

HOMER

(*Turning to Ida*)
All of it. Why hasn't Myrtle a home and been living up there in
my house all this time? What's it all about that I'm forty years
old and still living here and not having a home of my own?

IDA

But that's what you've always wanted, Homer.

HOMER

(*Accusingly*)
Why have I wanted it? I'm a man.

IDA

Of course, Homer.

HOMER

Then what's it all about? Myrtle cried half the night last night. I
heard her. And then my father leaves home. And then they take
our beautiful house away from us. So what's it all about?

IDA

(Rising)

I'm so sorry, Homer.

HOMER

(Crossing to Left exit)

I've got to think these things out. That's what I've got to do. I've got to think these things out.

(Exits)

IDA

(Following—and Off)

Oh, dear. Oh, dear—

(David and Carl come out of house Left. They are loaded with suitcases, tools, etc. Carl eagerly listens to David)

DAVID

Of course, it's just a supposition, Carl. But . . .

(Puts bags down Left Center—Carl does same)

Let us suppose that right now, at this moment, you *are* a dentist. Let's assume that.

CARL

(Eagerly)

All right, David, all right.

DAVID

You have your office. All your instruments, your chair, your tools—

CARL

X-ray machine.

DAVID

X-ray machine. Everything. And you're working on a patient. And suddenly do you know what you're going to say to yourself?

CARL

What?

DAVID

WHERE AM I? What am I doing here? I'm caught! I'm *Carl Bolton!* Where am I? Just as you do now—and how are you going to answer yourself? You can't say: Where am I? I'm a dentist. *What* am I, yes. But that's not what you ask yourself, Carl. You ask yourself: *Where* am I? Where am I in *life?* What's the meaning of it? And that's a very natural question, Carl. It's a question that a man like you must inevitably ask himself.

CARL

Is it really, David?

DAVID

Of course. The only reason you think it strange, that anyone thinks it's strange, is because the people you have been in contact with have never let that problem worry them. They are content to answer the question: "Where am I?" by: "I'm a dentist." And why shouldn't they? After all, it doesn't much matter where they are, does it?

CARL

(*Eagerly*)

But the answer, David. What's the answer?

DAVID

Ah, that's another thing. That's what we must find out.

CARL

If I could only find out that answer—

DAVID

We'll talk about it, Carl. We'll talk about it. Well, shall we get started?

(*Ida enters Left—Esther comes out of house and down steps*)

CARL

Yes, yes.

(*They start to load each other with the bags and tools*)

IDA

(*Tearfully*)

Carl, I've always been a good wife to you. I've always been faithful and—

(Turning to Esty)
Esty, what are we going to do?

ESTHER

(Crossing down steps—sitting on porch ledge)
I don't know what *you're* going to do, Ida. But I know what *I'm*
going to do.

IDA

What?

ESTHER

I'm going to sit right here and sort of bask in the sun.
(David looks up, surprised)

IDA

But they're going to leave us, Esty.

ESTHER

Well, let them! For heaven's sakes let them go and find out
where they are once and for all. If they get to be as old as they
are without knowing, the Lord knows it's high time for them to
find out.

DAVID

You see, Carl, as I was saying, there are some people who never
ask themselves the question: Where am I?

ESTHER

There're some people who don't have to. I *know* where *I* am. I'm
on the second floor. And to tell the truth, I'm beginning to like
the idea pretty well.

DAVID

Well, I'm glad if the arrangement pleases you, Esther.

ESTHER

It does. I've had more fun last night and today than I've had for
a long time.

DAVID

Ah, yes. Your games and so forth—

ESTHER

That's right. I like games. With lots of people on both sides.

DAVID

Ah, yes. Well, you're a free agent now, Esther.

ESTHER

I know I am. When I sat outside that locked door a few minutes ago waiting for you two to come out, I suddenly said to myself: "There's no fool like an old fool," and I was thinking of you and Carl. And then I said it again and it suddenly meant *me*. For fifty years I've washed and cooked and brought up children, and now suddenly I've got a chance to be free. I can come down here any time I want to, can go to the movies with the girls—do anything.
(*She stretches*)
It's nice!
(*Pause. David stands looking at her. Suddenly he turns to Carl*)

DAVID

Well, Carl, we'd better get back to the bathroom.

CARL

(*Picking up tools*)
All right, David. I'll come down and see you, Ida.
(*Starts Up Center*)

IDA

(*Following*)
I never thought you'd leave me, Carl.

CARL

I never thought I would either, Ida, but—
(*They exit Up Center*)

DAVID

(*Starts out—then turns back to Esther*)
You'll be occupying the second floor tonight?

ESTHER

I haven't decided yet. I may stay down here. Thor says I can stay as long as I like.

DAVID

Ah!

ESTHER

But I'll be quiet if I come in late.
  (*He stands looking at her for a second*)

DAVID

Well, pleasant dreams, Esther.

ESTHER

Thank you.
  (*He starts out—stops and turns*)

DAVID

I meant to say, if you prefer the lower floor to the upper—

ESTHER

No, I think I prefer the upper.

DAVID

I thought perhaps the stairs—

ESTHER

The stairs won't bother me any.

DAVID

That's fine.
  (*He hesitates a minute*)
If there is any rearrangement of furniture you wish done, Carl
and I will be glad to help you.

ESTHER

Thank you, David.

DAVID

There's no use straining yourself.

ESTHER

No.

DAVID

Well, good morning, Esther.

ESTHER

Good morning, David.

(*David exits up path. Esther watches him go, amused. Suddenly she starts to sing softly*)

Oh, sole mio—Ti-di-di-di-di—Ti-di-di-di-di—

(*Cora comes out of Ida's house. She crosses down the steps and walks Center to the path, waving the lease at Esty as she goes*)

CORA

Hello, Esty. All signed!

ESTHER

Where are you going!

CORA

(*Stopping*)

I'm going down the street to see Harold Blake. To see if we can use his truck. Maybe he can move us up there after work tomorrow or the next day.

(*Slightly malicious*)

You see, Esty, I've decided you're right. It *is* hard to go away and leave a house you've lived in so long—all the furniture and all— So I've decided to take some furniture along. Just Thor's chair so he won't be lonesome—and a couple of pieces out of the bedroom—Arry won't miss those. My goodness, Arry's got the whole house to live in. Isn't that right, Esty?

(*Esther has been looking at her steadily. She doesn't reply*)

Well, good-bye, Esty, and if anybody wants to make trouble, they can.

(*She starts out between the houses—airily—and meets Ida coming in. She greets her effusively*)

Hello, Ida.

(*She exits—Ida crosses to Esty*)

ESTHER

(*Rises—grabs Ida tensely*)

Ida!

IDA

What?

ESTHER

Cora's going through with this house thing, and you know what's going to happen, don't you?
(*Crossing Right*)
Arry's mad enough to do anything.

IDA

Well, what can we do about it?

ESTHER

What do you suppose Arry would do if we told her we knew about her and Thor?

IDA

(*Shocked*)
It would be awfully hard on Arry.

ESTHER

Not as hard as it will be on everybody if she starts to make trouble.
(*Suddenly*)
Let's go in and talk to Arry before Cora gets back.
(*She starts drawing Ida toward the house*)

IDA

But Thor's in there.

ESTHER

We'll get her out here then. We'll get her out if we have to drag her out.

IDA

All right—Oh, dear! It never rains but it pours.
(*They start in. Myrtle comes out house Left*)

MYRTLE

Oh, good morning, Mrs. Bolton.

IDA

(*Stops—comes down steps*)
Oh! Oh, good morning, Myrtle. Are you up?

MYRTLE

Yes, I am.

ESTHER

Good morning, Myrtle.

MYRTLE

Good morning. Isn't it lovely out?

ESTHER

Yes, isn't it?
        (*To Ida*)
I'll go in. Come in as soon as you can.

IDA

All right.
        (*Esther goes in*)
Well, you had a pretty good sleep, didn't you?

MYRTLE

I guess you think I'm a dreadful laggard, staying in bed so long?

IDA

Not at all. I'm glad you did.

MYRTLE

I don't always do it!

IDA

I bet you don't. And I'll bet you're good and hungry, too.

MYRTLE

No. I helped myself to some coffee and a little toast.

IDA

But you'll want more than that.

MYRTLE

I couldn't, really. That was just what I wanted.

IDA

Are you sure?

MYRTLE

Yes, really.

IDA

Well, if you're sure.
   (*Ida makes a move to start in*)

MYRTLE

Oh, is Homer—around?

IDA

Why, I wonder where he got to—Homer?
   (*Homer enters Stage Left*)

HOMER

Here I am.

IDA

Oh! I thought you'd gone in.

MYRTLE

Good morning, Homer.

HOMER

Good morning, Myrtle.

MYRTLE

Isn't it a lovely day?

HOMER

Sure is.

MYRTLE

My, you can feel the sun on you as warm as toast. I thought
maybe you'd like to take a little walk?

HOMER

I'd like to.

MYRTLE

That's the first thing I thought of when I woke this morning, and
saw the sunshine. I thought, Homer and I will take a nice walk
this morning, till train time. Maybe we'll go up and look at our
new house even.
   (*Embarrassed pause*)

HOMER

Well—

MYRTLE

Of course if you don't want to—

HOMER

(*Stepping toward her*)
No, it isn't that. I—All right.

IDA

That's right. Now you take a nice walk and be back for lunch.
Now I've got to run over to Cora's for a minute if you'll excuse
me.

MYRTLE

Oh, of course.

IDA

You're sure you don't want any more breakfast?

MYRTLE

(*Brightly*)
Honest Injun!
        (*Ida enters house Right—Pause. Homer waits awkwardly.
        Myrtle turns to him with a bright smile*)
Hello.

HOMER

Hello.

MYRTLE

Did you have a good sleep?

HOMER

Not very.

MYRTLE

Oh, what a shame. I slept ever so nicely.

HOMER

Did you?

MYRTLE

That's the softest bed I think I ever slept on.

HOMER

I thought about things all night.

MYRTLE

Now you shouldn't have done that. I told you when you went to bed that you were to go right to sleep and not think about anything.

HOMER

(*Turns away*)
I couldn't help it.

MYRTLE

That was bad of you.

HOMER

(*Turns toward her*)
Myrtle.

MYRTLE

(*Stopping him*)
Now don't you feel bad about anything, Homer. I thought it all out this morning. I see just what you mean about not leaving your mother. And I think it's nice of you.

HOMER

No, it's not that. It's something else.

MYRTLE

What?

HOMER

It's—something I've got to tell you before we go. It wouldn't be fair not to.

MYRTLE

What is it?
(*She waits—Homer hesitates*)

HOMER

It's not very nice.

MYRTLE

My goodness, it can't be so very bad. Now out with it.

HOMER

It's about our house.

MYRTLE

(*Suddenly alarmed*)

Nothing's happened to it, Homer! It hasn't burned down or anything—?

HOMER

No, it's—all right.

MYRTLE

(*Her hand to her heart*)

My goodness, you scared me. You shouldn't say things like that.

HOMER

It's just that—it isn't our house anymore.

(*Pause. Myrtle looks at him, puzzled*)

MYRTLE

Our house—isn't our house anymore?

HOMER

My father just rented it to Aunt Cora. She's got a twenty-year
lease on it.

MYRTLE

On *our* house?

HOMER

Uh-huh. I guess he thought we weren't going to be using it.

(*Myrtle, bewildered, puts her hand to her head. She turns
away slightly, too stunned to understand it yet. Homer
watches her. Anguished*)

Gee, Myrtle, I'm so sorry!

MYRTLE

(*In a dazed voice*)
It's all right. Of course, it's all right—It really wasn't our house,
was it? Not really. It was your father's house. You couldn't
expect him to just keep it empty until—He has kept it empty for
five years—You couldn't expect—
(*She turns away from him—trying to reason it out—and
to keep back the tears*)

HOMER

(*Stepping toward her*)
I'll build you one myself, Myrtle. I'll build you a house that'll
make that house look like a garage.

MYRTLE

Don't be silly!
(*She moves over by stump*)

HOMER

(*Crossing to chair Left—sitting*)
Myrtle—I've been thinking things out.

MYRTLE

(*Wearily*)
Yes, you said you had.
(*Sits on stump*)

HOMER

Not just last night. Today, too. I ought to have got married and
had a home of my own a long time ago. I ought to have done it.

MYRTLE

(*Faintly*)
Why didn't you, Homer?

HOMER

I got caught. Somehow or other I got caught. But I'd do it now,
Myrtle. I'd do it now except—
(*Rises. Crosses Center*)

MYRTLE

Except what?

HOMER

Except now I really have to stay here with my mother.

MYRTLE

(*Pause—then suddenly turns to him*)
Homer! Do you mean you really want to marry me now?
(*Rising and crossing to him—rapidly*)
Because if you do—if you really want to—it doesn't matter about
our house—and you could be with your mother too. I could come
and live here with you in this house. And we could have your lit-
tle room. It's a darling little room. I looked at it on the way
down. And we could all be together.
(*Homer turns to her—she pauses*)
That is, if you *wanted* to, of course.

HOMER

You mean, you'd live here—with everybody?

MYRTLE

Of course I would. I'd just love it.

HOMER

You always said a woman wanted a home of her own.

MYRTLE

Well, I'd be having it. It'd be even nicer in one way than being
up there on Sycamore Drive. We'd never be lonesome here.
(*Pause. Homer rises*)

HOMER

(*Suddenly*)
I'm awfully fond of you, Myrtle.

MYRTLE

Are you, Homer?

HOMER

I'm fonder of you than anything I could think of.
(*Pause, he stands looking at her*)
I think you're wonderful.
(*They stand looking at each other a minute*)

MYRTLE

Thank you, Homer.

> (*Myrtle looks away a minute—starts to say something—*
> *then changes her mind—looks back*)

Shall we take our walk?

> (*Homer comes to her. He starts to put his arm around her.*
> *Hesitates. Looks over at the other house. Puts his arm*
> *around her anyway. They exit Up Center.—The door of*
> *the house at Right opens and Esther comes out. She has*
> *hold of Arry's hand and is pulling her. Arry is drawing*
> *back*)

ARRY

What do you want to talk to me about?

ESTHER

Oh, come on, Arry. We're not going to hurt you.

ARRY

> (*Drawing back*)

I don't trust you, Esty. When you start talking—

> (*She suddenly comes out with a rush. Ida, who has given*
> *her a push, appears in the door behind her—steps to the*
> *Right of her*)

Hey! Quit that! What'd you push me for?

IDA

I didn't push you.

ARRY

You did too.

IDA

I just wanted to come out and you were blocking the way.

ARRY

What's going on here anyway?

> (*They are at each side of her—She looks from one to the*
> *other*)

I'm going back in.

> (*She starts to duck into the house. Ida grabs one arm—*
> *Esther the other*)

ESTHER

Oh, no, you're not.

IDA

You're coming right along with us.

ARRY

(*Struggling*)
You let go of me. Let go of me!

ESTHER

Oh, be quiet, Arry.

ARRY

Let go of me!
(*Screaming*)
Let go of me!

ESTHER

Oh, my goodness. Let go of her, Ida.
(*They let go of Arry*)

ARRY

Thank you. Thank you so much.
(*She starts up steps*)

ESTHER

Go on back in. If you don't want to hear what we have to say, you don't need to.

ARRY

(*Stops—turns slowly*)
I didn't say I wouldn't like to hear what you had to say, Esty, but when one person wishes to talk to another, there are certain rules of nice behavior they try to observe.

ESTHER

(*Trying not to giggle*)
I'm sorry, Arry.

ARRY

I doubt very much whether in the best society you would find one person approaching the back of another person and pushing them from behind.

IDA

I'm sorry, Arry. We just wanted to have a little talk with you. Of course, if you don't care to—

ARRY

I'd be very glad to.
          (*She walks over to the stump, sits. Faces Esther and Ida*)
Well, Esther!

ESTHER

Well, Arry, I'll tell you. It's about Thor and Cora moving up to Homer's house—
          (*Arry jumps up and starts to run in*)

ARRY

Oh, no, you don't! I know you, Esty!

ESTHER

          (*As she and Ida stop Arry*)
Now wait a minute, Arry.

ARRY

          (*Between them*)
I don't want to talk about it.

IDA

You *got* to talk about it.

ARRY

I knew I shouldn't have trusted you—

ESTHER

Why? What do you think we're going to say?

ARRY

You're going to say Thor and Cora ought to move up there.

ESTHER

Well, don't you think they should?

ARRY

No, I don't.

IDA

Why not?

ARRY

Just because I don't, that's all.

ESTHER

But if Cora wants to—and Thor wants to—

ARRY

Thor doesn't want to.

IDA

How do you know?

ARRY

(*Hesitating*)
Well, I—I don't think he does—

ESTHER

Why, have you talked to him?

ARRY

Well, I—Not much.

ESTHER

Then you're not sure, are you?

ARRY

No, I'm not sure—

IDA

Then if he does want to and Cora wants to—why, it would be pretty nice for them, don't you think?
(*Arry, trapped, moves back to the stump. They watch her*)

ARRY

(*Sullenly—sits*)
I don't know what business it is of yours anyway.

ESTHER

Strictly speaking, I don't suppose it is. But after all, we're sisters. And it means so much to Cora . . . I'm just thinking of her happiness.

ARRY

And what about *my* happiness?

ESTHER

Well, in this case, certainly Cora's happiness is the one to consider.

ARRY

I don't see why.

ESTHER

Don't you? Cora wants to live alone with Thor, Arry.

ARRY

(*Suddenly vicious*)
Well, she's not going to!

IDA

Oh, isn't she?

ARRY

Over my dead body she is. If they try anything there's a few things I can tell—

IDA

You've made that threat a lot of times, Arry—

ARRY

I mean it.

ESTHER

What could you tell, Arry?

ARRY

Plenty.

ESTHER

What could you tell that all of us don't already know? That we haven't all known for years?
(*Sudden pause. Arry looks up at Esther, startled*)

ARRY

(*Softly*)
What do you mean, Esty?

(*She looks at Ida, frightened, and back at Esther. In a whisper*)
What do you mean?

IDA

Do you think we're all blind, Arry?

ESTHER

Don't you think all of us know by this time about you and Thor?
(*Pause*)

ARRY

(*Frightened*)
No—no—Esty—

IDA

We've all known for years. All of us.

ARRY

No—no—

ESTHER

But we've all kept our mouths shut for Cora's sake. If you want to make a nasty business out of it, go on and do it. But it won't get you anywhere, Arry. And you won't look so nice, carrying on for years with the husband of your own sister right under her very nose—

ARRY

(*Shocked—rises*)
Esty! Esty, what do you mean? You don't think—Ida, you don't think—that Thor and me—all this time—Oh, my God!
(*She buries her face in her hands. Ida and Esther watch uneasily*)

IDA

What do you mean, Arry?

ARRY

(*Moaning—sits on stump*)
Oh, my God! Oh, my God!

ESTHER

(*Uneasily*)

But you've always hinted in front of everyone, Arry—

ARRY

You've all thought that Thor and me—all these years—does Cora think that?

ESTHER

I don't know, Arry. Nobody's ever said anything to Cora. I guess Cora doesn't think anything.

ARRY

(*Suddenly she turns toward the house. Rises, and yells with a sudden frenzied frightenedness*)

Thor! Thor! Thor!

(*Esther and Ida move Down Right*)

Thor! Thor!

THOR

(*Hurries out of the house Right*)

What's the matter? What's the matter, Arry?

ARRY

They say that—they think that—

(*Cora has entered between the houses. She stops, frozen, watching the scene*)

CORA

Why, Arry, what's the matter?

(*Arry hesitates a minute—looks at Cora—then suddenly runs into the house, weeping*)

THOR

What's the matter with her?

ESTHER

(*Starting into house*)

I don't quite know. I'll find out.

THOR

What did you say to her, Esty?

CORA

(*Hard*)
Yes. What did you say to her?

ESTHER

(*Looking at Cora*)
We just had a little fuss, Cora.

CORA

About what?
    (*Pause. Esty looks at Cora*)

ESTHER

I'll tell you later.
    (*She exits*)

CORA

Thor!
    (*He turns and sees her watching him*)
I wonder what she could have said to Arry?

THOR

I don't know, Cora. Maybe she said something Arry didn't like so much.

CORA

Yes, she must have. I wonder what it could have been?

THOR

I don't know, Cora.
    (*Pause. Cora turns to Ida brightly*)

CORA

Ida, has Carl still got those packing cases he used to have in his garage?

IDA

(*Mystified*)
Why—I don't know, Cora—

CORA

Harold Blake hasn't got any. He says he can move Thor and me up day after tomorrow, but he just hasn't got any packing cases.
    (*Thor looks at her startled*)

THOR

(*Hesitantly*)
Day after tomorrow?

CORA

Uh-huh!
(*To Ida*)
Can we go over and see if they're still there?
(*She has started Off Left*)

IDA

(*Following*)
Yes—of course—

THOR

But Cora—But Cora—
(*They go Off Left—Thor watches them. He sits on ledge
—depressed*)
The day after tomorrow! Good God!
(*Homer and Myrtle enter from between the houses. They
see Thor but he doesn't see them. Myrtle goes quickly into
Ida's house and Homer crosses to Thor*)

HOMER

Uncle Thor.

THOR

(*Startled*)
Oh, hello, Homer.

HOMER

I've got to talk to you, Uncle Thor.

THOR

Well, go ahead, Homer.

HOMER

It's about my house. I've got to have it back.

THOR

Well, by God, Homer, nobody wishes you had it back more than
I do.

HOMER

But I've got to have it back.

THOR

Well, there's no use talking to me about it. You'll have to talk to your Aunt Cora.

HOMER

No, I've got to talk to you about it. You see, last night when I thought my father was going to start having spells again—I felt I shouldn't leave my mother—and I told that to Myrtle and—

THOR

Yeah, I see the predicament, Homer, but—

HOMER

But this morning Myrtle said we could get married and live here with my mother and—

THOR

I know, Homer. That's kinda tough but—

HOMER

It isn't that so much but, you see—Myrtle just told me. She's going to have a—baby.
(*Pause. There is a complete, dead silence. Thor looks at Homer in complete and utter bewilderment*)

THOR

(*In a ghostly whisper*)
What?

HOMER

Uh-huh.

THOR

A—baby—?

HOMER

Uh-huh.

THOR

You mean—a—
>   (*He gestures with his hands*)
—baby—

HOMER

Uh-huh.

THOR

>   (*In a whisper, slowly looking Homer over*)

Well, for God's sakes!
>   (*He rises and walks around Homer, staring at him from all
>   angles. Homer stands, head down in embarrassment*)

Well, what the hell do you know about that!
>   (*Homer's head sinks lower*)

Well, I'll be Goddamned!
>   (*Suddenly Thor's face lights up with a great glow. He
>   beams at Homer. He shouts—*)

Well! Well!
>   (*He rubs his hands together, beaming at Homer*)

Well, well! Well, well! What the hell do you know about that!
>   (*Slaps Homer on the back*)

That's a pretty good one! Yes sir, by God, you certainly had your
old Uncle Thor fooled!

HOMER

>   (*Suddenly smiling, modestly*)

Just one of those things, you know.

THOR

Sure, sure!

HOMER

Don't really know how it happened.

THOR

By God, ain't it the truth.

HOMER

Kinda lose your head sometimes—

THOR

(*Clapping him on the back*)

Ain't it the truth. By God! Well, what the hell do you know about that!

CURTAIN

ACT III

ACT III

SCENE: *The same. A short time later. As the curtain rises, Cora is eagerly watching the expression on Esther's face, which is one of sheer blankness. Both are seated, on steps house Right, and chair Left of steps.*

ESTHER

Homer?

CORA

That's what he told Thor.

ESTHER

But it's not possible, Cora.

CORA

Seems it is.

ESTHER

A baby!

CORA

(*Nervously*)

Shh! For goodness' sakes, Esty, don't keep saying it. If Arry ever got hold of it, Ida would find out in a minute.

ESTHER

But I just don't understand. How did it happen?

CORA

How does it usually happen?

ESTHER

But Homer must have—must have—

CORA

Of course he must have. That's the point.

ESTHER

Must have been all this time—

CORA

Seven years—

ESTHER

Well, I give up. I've seen a lot of things in my time, Cora. First the telephone. Everybody said it wouldn't work.

CORA

(Giggling)

Now stop it, Esty! Somebody'll hear you. Besides, it's an awful thing.

ESTHER

Of course it's an awful thing.

CORA

If Arry should ever find out—

ESTHER

What are they going to do about it?

CORA

Well, they're going to get married—

ESTHER

I know, but even so—

CORA

Oh, they'll take a trip somewhere when the time comes. There's no hurry. Now for goodness' sakes, you mustn't let on to Thor that I told you. I promised him I wouldn't.

ESTHER

Does Homer know you know?

CORA

Nobody knows, Esty! *Nobody!* Thor promised Homer he wouldn't breathe it to a soul.

ESTHER

But why *did* Homer tell Thor?

CORA

Well—
  (*She rises—crosses Down Right—hesitates. Suddenly she reverts to the grim attitude she had in the previous act*)
He wants his house back.

ESTHER
  (*Looking at her quickly*)
Oh! I see.

CORA

I've just had a talk with Thor. He says I've got to let them have it.

ESTHER

Well, I suppose he feels if they're going to have a baby—

CORA
  (*Turns to Esty*)
That's not the reason Thor wants me to give it back. Is it, Esty?

ESTHER

What do you mean, Cora?

CORA

You know what I mean. Thor's afraid to move up there with me.

ESTHER
  (*Rises—crosses to Cora*)
Cora, I'd like to ask you something.

CORA

What?

ESTHER

Have you ever doubted that Thor loved you?
(*Cora is not prepared for this. She is rather surprised.
She thinks it over*)

CORA

Why—no—

ESTHER

Have you ever doubted that you came first—always—with Thor?

CORA

(*After a moment*)
No—I've never doubted that—

ESTHER

And you know you always will come first?

CORA

Yes—

ESTHER

Well, that's something to be able to say after fifty years of marriage, isn't it?

CORA

(*Slowly*)
Yes, it's something. It's a *lot*. If that's all you can get.
(*She turns away. Esther watches her*)
Well, I better go in. Now for goodness' sakes, Esty, don't let on
to Thor.

ESTHER

Let on what? Oh, about the baby!

CORA

(*Motioning her to be quiet*)
Esty! Esty!

ESTHER

(*In a whisper—sitting*)

All right. All right.

(*Cora stands quietly a moment*)

CORA

Anyway, it'll be nice to have a baby in the family again, won't it?

ESTHER

Real nice.

(*Cora starts in as Thor comes out of the house at left, followed by Ida, Myrtle and Homer. Esther and Cora watch Myrtle*)

THOR

(*As he comes down the steps*)

What you want to do, Homer, is to take a nice long honeymoon. To hell with these picky little two, three week affairs. Months, I say, even if you have to wait a few months before you can get away.

HOMER

That sounds like a good idea, Uncle Thor.

THOR

You bet it's a good idea. Pick some nice quiet place and just settle down and live there awhile. Get to know each other. Come on, we'll dig up that atlas and have a look—Oop! Watch out there! Take it easy!

(*He catches Myrtle by the arm and helps her down the steps*)

MYRTLE

Oh, thank you.

THOR

(*Carefully walking her Center*)

Bad step there—Well, Esty, old girl, have you heard the news?

ESTHER

(*Startled*)

Why—I—I thought it was a se—

(*She glances at Cora*)

CORA

(*Quickly*)

Homer and Myrtle are going to be married.

THOR

(*Chuckling—standing between Homer and Myrtle*)

Yes, sir, gonna tie them up tighter'n a drumstick.

ESTHER

Congratulations, Homer.

HOMER

Thank you, Aunt Esther.

(*Thor has crossed Center Right*)

ESTHER

I'm sure you'll be very happy, Myrtle.

MYRTLE

Well, I just guess I will be. My goodness, I'm about as happy
right now as a girl has any right to be. Everybody's being so nice
it just—hurts.

THOR

Well, they better be nice! Aren't you going to congratulate them,
Cora?

CORA

(*Who has been absorbed looking over Myrtle for evi-
dence*)

Of course I am. Congratulations, Homer.

(*There is a slight pause. Homer looks at her sullenly. Then
turns away*)

HOMER

(*Gruffly*)

Thank you.

(*Cora is disturbed. The others watch her*)

CORA

(*Flustered—after pause*)

Well, well, I know you're going to be very happy, Myrtle.

MYRTLE

Well, I do, too. I just guess I will be. My goodness, I'm almost as happy right this minute as any girl—It isn't every day a girl gets a proposal of marriage. I just guess we'll be happy, won't we, Homer?

HOMER

Might be happy if we had a house to live in.

(*There is a dead pause. All eyes are focussed on Cora. She becomes very flustered and turns away*)

MYRTLE

Now you stop talking about that, Homer. My goodness, we can get along without that house. We'll be so happy right here in this house that you're going to be astounded.

HOMER

I don't want to live in this house.

MYRTLE

Well, we're going to. Now you stop striking discordant notes, Homer. We're just going to change the subject and not revert to it again. We'll just change the subject—er—

(*Pause. They all wait for her to do it*)

Did you hear what Mother Ida said?

(*She crosses to stump*)

ESTHER

No. What did Mother Ida say?

MYRTLE

She said she didn't feel so much as if she was losing a son but more like she was gaining a daughter.

ESTHER

Did Mother Ida say that?

MYRTLE

Yes, she did.
(*Sits on stump*)

IDA

(*Sadly*)
It isn't going to be so easy though—

HOMER

(*Firmly*)
Now, Mother, none of that. I've made up my mind.

IDA

(*Timidly*)
Oh, I know you have, Homer. And I'm so glad. I just meant if you shouldn't live here it isn't going to be so easy—with your father gone—

HOMER

I'll speak to my father, but it isn't going to influence me. I've made up my mind. Myrtle and I are going to be married and we're going to live alone. If we can find some old house. Just us two.

THOR

By God, that's all right for awhile, Homer, but you can't keep a marriage down to two forever, you know.

MYRTLE

(*Giggling nervously*)
Oh, you!

IDA

Well, there's plenty of time to think of that later.

THOR

(*Roaring*)
By God, that's a fact, Ida. Plenty of time for that later.
(*He nudges Homer and gives him a knowing wink*)

MYRTLE

Well, my goodness, we're certainly crossing our bridges—

HOMER

(*Firmly*)

If I should ever have a son, I won't let him stay around the house after he's nineteen.

IDA

Homer!

HOMER

I won't, Mother. There's no use arguing. At nineteen he gets out.

MYRTLE

Homer!

HOMER

Animals, too. You don't see an animal hanging around home after it's grown up, do you?

THOR

No, sir, you don't, Homer. That's a fact.

HOMER

(*To Esther*)

Did you ever hear of a grown male dog who wouldn't leave his mother?

ESTHER

I don't think I ever did, Homer.

HOMER

(*To Ida*)

Did you ever hear of *any* animal that wouldn't get out when he grew up?

IDA

I—I don't know, Homer—

HOMER

Even pigs. The mother pushes them out right away. And that's the way it ought to be.

MYRTLE

(*To them all*)

It's very interesting, isn't it?

IDA

(Tearfully)
I'm sure I never tried to do anything to hold Homer—

MYRTLE

(Crossing to her quickly)
Well, I should just guess you didn't either—

IDA

I always tried to push him out—

MYRTLE

Of course you did. Now we won't have any more talk like this!
Don't you say anything more, Homer. My goodness, I guess I can
realize how your mother feels!

HOMER

Well, every animal *I* ever heard of—

MYRTLE

Homer!

IDA

(Tearfully)
Oh!
          (She runs into house Left)

MYRTLE

Oh, Mother Ida—He didn't mean—
          (She turns to Homer)
My goodness, Homer, I just don't know what's got into you! You
used to always be so nice to your mother. You just seem to be
striking discordant notes all the time. Pigs, indeed! You're getting
just terrible, Homer!

THOR

(Crossing Right)
Well, come on. Let's get this honeymoon figured out. Where do
you suppose that atlas is, Cora?
          (They all look at Cora)

CORA

(*Crossing Center—strangely grim*)

I don't know.

THOR

(*Uneasily*)

Well, come on. We'll find it.

(*As they start in Arry comes out. They all stop suddenly and look at her. Cora watches her. Tentatively*)

Hello, Arry. Headache gone?

ARRY

I want to talk to you a minute, Thor.

THOR

(*Uneasily*)

Well, we were just going in and—

ARRY

I guess you can spare me a few minutes.

(*Slight pause. Thor is uneasy. Arry starts down the steps*)

THOR

Well, all right, Arry.

ARRY

Thank you.

(*She crosses Down to Esty*)

THOR

Look in the bottom of the victrola, Homer. I think the atlas's in there. I'll be in in a minute.

(*Myrtle and Homer exit. Arry reaches Esther. There is a feeling of tension. Arry hands Esther a letter*)

ARRY

I want you to read this sometime, Esty.

ESTHER

What is it?

ARRY

You'll find out.

ESTHER

All right, Arry.
(*She eyes her a moment sharply*)
Is your head better?

ARRY

My head's all right.

ESTHER

Good.
(*Arry turns to Cora, who has been watching her*)

ARRY

(*Suddenly*)
Don't you worry. You won't have to bother with me anymore.
Just don't you worry.
(*A moment's pause. They stand looking at each other*)

CORA

(*After a moment, quietly*)
Arry wants to talk to Thor, Esty. Would you take a little walk
with me?
(*Esther and Cora go out between the houses in silence.
Thor looks after them a moment, uneasily, and then he
goes to Arry who has seated herself and sits looking quietly
into space*)

THOR

(*Uneasily*)
You oughtn't to say things like that to Cora, Arry. No use getting
her any madder than she is.
(*He looks at her. She is paying no attention*)
And what did you mean by she won't have to bother with you
anymore?
(*She doesn't answer. Thor looks at her, uneasy*)
(*With fake cheerfulness*)
Anyway, I think everything's going to turn out fine.

(*He sits by her on the lower step—Pause. Arry has not moved—Thor is still uneasy*)

All of us got a little excited—but, hell, what's the difference. Nobody meant what they said.

(*Pause. He eyes her*)

Anything the matter, Arry?

ARRY

(*After a moment*)

What does it mean to you to grow old, Thor?

(*Thor looks at her in surprise*)

THOR

What do you mean, Arry?

ARRY

Doesn't getting old mean that—well, that things don't trouble you so much anymore? That everything's more peaceful and quiet—

THOR

Peaceful and quiet! I guess that must be when you get *real* old, Arry. Say in your late eighties.

ARRY

I always thought of getting old sort of like going to bed when you're nice and drowsy—and yet you know you won't fall to sleep for a little while yet—and you just lie there sort of comfortably—and enjoy it—But it isn't that way at all.

THOR

I don't know what you're getting at, Arry.

ARRY

Well, I've been lying down thinking.

(*She turns to him suddenly*)

You've been real good to me, Thor. You're a real good man.

THOR

(*Embarrassed*)

Oh, hell, Arry.

ARRY

I mean it. Cora too. I want you to know I appreciate the way
you've had me in your home all these years.

THOR

It was your home too, Arry.

ARRY

Nope. That's what I found out. It wasn't ever my home. I
haven't got a home. That's what I mean about getting old. I
guess it's nice and peaceful if you got a home. If you got a husband. If you got somebody to get old with—But I haven't. So
you know what I'm going to do, Thor?

THOR

What, Arry?

ARRY

I'm going to go away.

THOR

What do you mean?

ARRY

I'm leaving. I'm leaving you and Cora to have a home together.

THOR

But, Arry—

ARRY

No, Thor, I'm going to do it. I should have done it years
ago, but I didn't. I'm going to try to forget you, Thor.

THOR

Gee, Arry, I don't know what to say.

ARRY

There's nothing to say.
        (*Arry rises and crosses to steps*)
Thor.

THOR

Yeah?

> ARRY

When I die—you know what I want on my stone?

> THOR

What?

> ARRY

"Home is the sailor, home from the sea
And the hunter, home from the hill."

> THOR

All right, Arry.

> ARRY

Mama used to say that—Now I'll go in and pack.
>   (*Goes up stairs—at top—turns*)
Thor.
>   (*He turns*)
I'm not sorry about anything.

> THOR

All right, Arry.

> ARRY

Not sorry at all.
>   (*She exits. Thor looks after her, sadly*)

> THOR

>   (*Rising—going up steps*)
Poor Arry! All alone in the world.
>   (*Thor stands looking after her a moment. He stops as
>   David and Carl enter, loaded down with Carl's luggage
>   and tools as they were when they left. Thor, unnoticed,
>   watches them. David puts bags on the porch—Carl leaves
>   his Down Left*)

> DAVID

For example, if you were taken blindfolded to some part of the
city and the blindfold were taken off, how would you find out
where you were?

> CARL

I'd look to see what street I was on.

DAVID

Exactly. Now say there wasn't any sign.—Or say you were lost in a woods. At night. How would you find out where you were?

(*Thor shakes his head, and exits*)

CARL

Well, I know the North star. And I could wander around until I found some landmark I knew and get my location that way—

DAVID

All right. Now to find your location in life, Carl, you do the same thing. Just wander around until you find a few landmarks. A man like you has got to make it his business to find his own location among the concepts that we know. He has got to search himself, search all the knowledge that he has, all the knowledge that others have until the last blade of grass in that lawn, or the last pebble in that road bears some relation to him, takes on some meaning, becomes a landmark so he knows just where he is. Only then is a man like you safe; when you can say, "I am eight miles north of water; I am three thoughts under love; I am ten beats past despair," then you'll know where you are, Carl.

(*David pauses and looks at Carl*)

Do you understand what I mean, Carl?

CARL

Well—I don't *quite* understand, David.

DAVID

(*Thoughtfully—crossing Left*)

Well, there's an *idea* there, Carl.

CARL

(*Eagerly*)

I know there is, David.

DAVID

(*Turning to Carl*)

Yes, there's an idea there *somewhere*, if we can pin it down. Well, let's pin it down, Carl. Let's pin it down.

CARL

All right, David. Let's!

> (*Esther comes in between the houses Center to stump—
> David breaks off*)

DAVID

Ah, Esther.

ESTHER

I thought it was you, David.

DAVID

Yes, Esther, it is I.

CARL

We're—we're bringing my things back.

ESTHER

Yes, I see. There's nothing wrong, is there?

CARL

Well, it's that little closet we were going to make into a bath. It's not very well located. It's not under the upstairs bathroom.

ESTHER

Yes, I could have told you that.

CARL

Well, it would cost nearly three hundred dollars to put it in shape.

ESTHER

As much as that? Oh, dear, dear!

CARL

We'd practically have to tear the whole house down.

ESTHER

I see. I see.

CARL

And as David says—the idea doesn't seem very practical.

ESTHER

Well, no, it certainly doesn't, does it?

CARL

And so—we're bringing my things back.
>*(Embarrassed pause)*
Well, I'll just take these out.
>*(He exits Left with tools. Esther stands watching David)*

ESTHER

Poor Carl. He seems upset.

DAVID

Upset? No—Fundamentally I should say Carl's a very sound person, Esther.

ESTHER

>*(Smiling)*
Really?

DAVID

Yes. He thinks things out very clearly—very logically.
>*(Pause. She stands regarding him, smiling. He is embarrassed. Starts to pick up bags)*
Well—

ESTHER

>*(Sits)*
David, I'd like to read you something.

DAVID

>*(Hesitating with bags in hand)*
Well, Esty, I—

ESTHER

You know what we've suspected about Arry and Thor all these years, don't you, David?

DAVID

>*(Turning)*
Oh, I've heard the talk, Esther. I never paid much attention to it.

ESTHER

Arry just gave me this letter.
>*(Shows the letter. David puts down bags and crosses to stump and sits)*

Do you remember—oh, it must have been all of forty years ago—after Arry had been living with them about a year—Cora had to go to the hospital for a couple of weeks?

DAVID

I think I do—vaguely—

ESTHER

Thor and Arry were alone. She was about seventeen. She didn't know much about anything. Right off the farm. She was pretty, full of life. You remember how Arry was. And—
    (*She reads*)
". . . and I don't know how it happened, Esty. I just don't. I loved Thor so much. I didn't realize it. I should have gone away, but I couldn't. We were both so miserable and scared. We didn't know what to do. But never after that time, Esty. Never. If Cora should ever know, I'd just die."
    (*Esther puts the letter down. They both sit thinking a moment*)
And so she just went on—living with them—because there wasn't any other place for her to go after that.
    (*Pause. She reads.*)
"When you and Ida told me what all of you had been thinking all this time—it seems to me I'd never be able to hold up my head again. It doesn't much matter about the years ahead—but it suddenly seemed as if all the years I've already lived didn't make much sense. I might just as well not have lived them."
    (*Pause. She puts the letter down*)

DAVID

    (*Rises—Moves Up Left*)
In the eyes of the world—I'm a failure—but we've kept our lives clear, Esther, and intelligent.

ESTHER

Yes, David, we have, haven't we?

DAVID

We've never let that other third element ever come in. We've kept ourselves to ourselves.

ESTHER

(*Smiling*)

Yes, I know what you mean by a Crystal Fortress, David.

(*He turns away. There is a moment's pause. Esther watches him, smiling*)

DAVID

It's a tragic line Aaronetta says about the years behind her "I might just as well not have lived them."

ESTHER

Yes.

DAVID

(*He turns to her, hesitating*)

Did you ever feel like that, Esther?

ESTHER

No, David.

DAVID

(*Eagerly*)

That's good.

ESTHER

But, you see, I always had you, David.

(*David is touched, embarrassed*)

DAVID

Thank you, Esther.

(*He turns to her with a smile and a short bow*)

Thank you. I'll take these in.

(*David goes in the house Left with bags. Esther rises and puts letter away as she sees Cora come down the path. Cora stops at the stump and stands looking ahead of her in silence*)

ESTHER

Well, Cora?

CORA

(*Quietly*)

I'm going to give Homer back his house.

ESTHER

(*Surprised*)
You are?

CORA

Yes. I've just been looking at it. I walked up there after you
left me. It's a beautiful house and Thor loves it—But as I stood
there looking at it I suddenly realized something. Living up there
alone with Thor is not what I'm after. *That's* not the important
thing. But there *is* something that's important and I'm going to
have it.
(*She turns away*)
I hate Arry!

ESTHER

No, Cora.

CORA

I hate her. But she can go on living with us. There's no other
place for her. But she's not going on living with us the way she
has been. Because I'm going to find out where I stand, Esty. And
I'm going to live alone with Thor in that very house—even with
Arry there.
(*After a moment*)
You remember that poem Papa used to say about us girls, Esty?
              "Esty's smartest,
               Arry's wildest,
               Ida's slowest,
               Cora's mildest."
And then he always used to look at me and say, "Poor Cora."
You remember that?

ESTHER

Yes.

CORA

(*Tensely*)
Well, I'm not "Poor Cora" anymore! There's such a thing as being
too mild!
(*Carl enters from the house Left. Comes down porch
steps*)

CARL

(*Hesitantly*)
Oh, Cora! I sort of hate to say anything to you about it but—

CORA

I'm giving Homer back his house, Carl.

CARL

(*Relieved*)
You are? Well, now that's awfully nice of you, Cora.
(*Crosses Left Center*)
Somehow I just knew you would.
(*Thor, Myrtle and Homer come out from the house at
Right. Cora watches them. Esther watches Cora*)

THOR

(*Crossing down steps*)
By God, that's just the place for you. Now why the hell do you
suppose I didn't think of that sooner?

MYRTLE

My goodness, it sounds simply heavenly.

THOR

You wait til you see that water coming down. And there's a little
boat that goes right out under the falls. Cora and I spent a whole
week there once.
(*David and Ida enter from house Left*)

HOMER

What do you think Myrtle?

MYRTLE

I think it sounds simply—divine!

HOMER

Then that settles it. That's where we'll go.

THOR

Hello, David. Heard the news?

DAVID

Ah, yes. My congratulations, Homer.
(*Ida crosses Down*)

HOMER

Thank you, Uncle David.

DAVID

I hope you're not being too impetuous.
(*Bowing to Myrtle*)
Myrtle, I hope—

MYRTLE

(*Crossing Down*)
My goodness, I just guess I will be. I'm just about as happy this
minute as any girl has a right to be—

CARL

Homer.

HOMER

Yes, Father?

CARL

Aunt Cora is giving you your house back.

HOMER

What?

MYRTLE

Our house!
(*They both look at Cora*)

CORA

(*Flustered*)
Yes, I—Of course, I guess I meant all along for you to have it
back—I—

MYRTLE

(*Crossing Center Left*)
Oh, I just think you are all the nicest people I ever met. I just
have never met so many nice people before. Aren't you going to
say anything, Homer?

HOMER
(*Crossing to Cora—kissing her*)
Well, thank you, Aunt Cora. Thank you ever so much.

CORA
Well—that's all right, Homer—

MYRTLE
I just feel like crying—
(*Arry comes out with hatbox and suitcase. She has on a large picture hat and looks very pretty. They all look at her. She poses at the top of steps for them. You see Cora stiffen and turn away. Esther watches her*)

THOR
By God, don't you look pretty, Arry.

ARRY
(*The great lady*)
Thank you, Thor.
(*Esty rises*)

IDA
Where are you going, Arry?
(*Pause. Arry comes down a step*)

ARRY
I'm moving out.
(*She looks around at them all*)

IDA
Moving?

ESTHER
Where are you going?

CARL
What do you mean, Arry?

MYRTLE
Why, Aunt Arry—?

ARRY

Yes, I'm leaving. I should have left years ago, of course, but I
didn't realize all the things I know now—
     (*Starts Center*)

ESTHER

Now, look here, Arry—

ARRY

Don't try to stop me, Esty. Please. It's a little upsetting, of
course, when you get to be my age to suddenly find out you're not
wanted anymore.

THOR

     (*Sorry*)
Ah, Arry—!

CORA

     (*Evenly*)
Let her finish, Thor.

ARRY

That all the years you thought you were a part of a home you
were really just sort of a—servant in it—and you could be dis-
missed when your services were no longer needed—
     (*Cross Center*)

THOR

By God, don't say that, Arry. You don't have to go anywhere.
     (*As Arry goes on Esty moves nearer Cora*)

ARRY

     (*With a little smile*)
But, Thor, I'm not wanted here.

THOR

You are, too. By God, this is your home, Arry. Isn't that so, Cora?

ARRY

Oh, don't ask Cora, Thor. Cora wants to live alone—She
doesn't want any sister of hers—

CORA

(*Starting toward Arry, furious*)
All right, Arry—I've stood—

ESTHER

(*Grabbing Cora*)
Wait a minute, Cora. Cora!
(*Cora turns and Esther hands her Arry's letter and motions for her to read it. Cora does so during the following scene. Arry turns to Myrtle*)

ARRY

I haven't had the opportunity to felicitate you on your approaching nuptials, Myrtle. I know you'll be very happy.

MYRTLE

Thank you, Aunt Arry.

ARRY

Homer too, of course.

HOMER

Thank you, Aunt Arry.

ARRY

But when you come right down to it, it's the woman that ought to be the happiest.

MYRTLE

I just guess that's the truth.

ARRY

She's the one who makes the home and looks after things and keeps it together.

MYRTLE

That's just the woman's function, I should think.
(*Cora has finished half the letter. She turns swiftly to Esther—Esty motions her to finish the letter—Cora moves to Thor's chair—sits*)

ARRY

And marriage gives a woman dignity, Myrtle. It gives her dignity and companionship and a place to be when she gets old. I know you'll be very happy, Myrtle.

MYRTLE

I know I will be.

ARRY

That's right.
> (*She turns. Cora has finished the letter and you see it has softened her. Arry and she look at each other. Arry is terrified and looks accusingly at Esty*)

Esty!
> (*Esty nods admittal that she gave Cora the letter. A moment's pause. Cora rises slowly. Crumples the letter and goes to Arry*)

CORA

You're going away, Arry.

ARRY

Yes, Cora.

CORA

> (*Touched*)

I'll—I'll miss you, Arry—
> (*Arry looks at her slowly*)

THOR

By God, you don't have to go, Arry.

ARRY

Yes, Thor, I must go. We'll see each other now and then, but I'm not going to live here anymore.

THOR

But where are you going to go?

ARRY

Well, I'm going to move over to Ida's—Ida told me years ago if I ever wanted to move over to her I could. Didn't you, Ida?

IDA

Of course, Arry.

CARL

Anytime you want to, Arry.

ARRY

(*Crossing between Ida and Carl*)

Well, now I want to. I want to spend the rest of the years with you.

(*Pause*)

HOMER

Well, if we're going to see our house we'd better go.

MYRTLE

Our house! My goodness! I've just never had so many people so nice to me all at once—

THOR

By God, Myrtle, if anybody isn't nice to you, just come to your old Uncle Thor.

MYRTLE

(*Crossing to Thor*)

Well, I certainly will. I'll just look on you as—well, as my—protector.

(*They laugh together*)

HOMER

(*Taking hold of Myrtle, gruffly*)

All right. That's enough. We better go now.

MYRTLE

Yes, Homer.

(*Homer leads Myrtle by the arm to the Right side of the Center path. He then firmly puts his arm around her waist and they exit Upstage Right.*

Arry looks at Carl who responds by picking up her bags and starting up to the Right porch. On the porch he adds his tool bag to his burden and starts into the house.

Ida crosses up to Arry and together they start up the porch steps. As they reach the top step, Ida moves Upstage to hold the screen door open. Arry hesitates at the porch column. She leans against it sensually and looks back longingly at Thor; then she breaks her own spell and goes into the house with Ida, inspecting the new surroundings as if she'd never seen them before.

Cora holds for long moment then she folds and crumples Arry's letter. She turns to look at Thor, smiles and slowly climbs the Left porch steps and goes in. Thor follows.

Both Esty and David have been watching the others exit with interest and amusement. Esty then turns her attention to David. He purposely avoids her glance and comes Downstage to the steps. He sits, looks front for a moment then—the decision made—looks at Esty as we go to black and)

CURTAIN